NEW PERSPECTIVES ON AMERICAN LITERATURE

Edited by
ISHTEYAQUE SHAMS

ATLANTIC
PUBLISHERS & DISTRIBUTORS

Published by
ATLANTIC PUBLISHERS AND DISTRIBUTORS
B-2, Vishal Enclave, Opp. Rajouri Garden, New Delhi-110027
Phones : 25413460, 25429987, 25466842

Sales Office
7/22, Ansari Road, Darya Ganj, New Delhi-110002
Phones : 23273880, 23275880, 23280451
Fax : 91-11-23285873
web : www.atlanticbooks.com
e-mail : info@atlanticbooks.com

ISBN 81-269-0393-7

Printed in India at
Nice Printing Press, Delhi

PREFACE

The present book has been prepared in the light of the need of the students of American Literature. The very first chapter entitled American Literature at a Glance gives the reader a clear conception of the growth of American Literature right from the beginning to the present day. In the subsequent chapters there are scholarly articles on American Women's Drama, Native North American Fiction, Recent American Poetry, Emerson, Whitman, John Updike, James Baldwin, John A. Williams, Saul Bellow, Toni Morrison, Katherine Anne Porter, Mark Strand and Richard Wright that make this book different from and more useful than the other books written on American Literature till date.

I am really thankful to all the contributors to this book for their well-researched and thought-provoking papers which will be very useful for teachers, scholars and students interested in American Literature.

I also thank my wife, Mumtaz Praveen and children Ashu and Sana for their co-operation by relieving me from family worries while preparing this book.

My sincere thanks are due to Dr. K.R. Gupta, Chairman, M/s Atlantic Publishers and Distributors, New Delhi, for his kind encouragement which enabled me to prepare this book.

ISHTEYAQUE SHAMS
Editor

CONTENTS

1

American Literature at a Glance

ISHTEYAQUE SHAMS

American literature begins with the orally transmitted myths, legends, tales and lyrics of Indian cultures. It is believed that there was no written literature among more than five hundred Indian languages and tribal cultures that existed in North America before the first Europeans arrived. As a result, Native American oral literature is quite diverse. Natives from quasi-nomadic huntic cultures like the Navajo are different from stories of settled agricultural tribes such as the pueblo-dwelling Acoma, the stories of northern lake side dwellers such as the Ojibwa often differ radically from stories of desert tribes like the Hopi.

American literature takes a new turn in the seventeenth century in a search for the ideal a search lighted and directed by hope and expectation. This search has been persistently a part of the entire history of the literature growing out of the impact of European civilization upon the developing American frontier. This literature has never been removed from involvement in the human situation. It has indicated concern and compassion, even in its analysis and its evaluation. Intolerable injustice, social blindness, or brutalization conditions have been brought before the bar of public conscience by writers feeling a responsibility to brotherhood and the integrity of the self.

Though some writers of the post world war period have seemed to falter, the weight of the American literary tradition has held confidently to a vision of a man based on a conception of justice and the value and unlimited potential of the individual whose essential dignity is not betrayed. A trust in men is apparent in the social and political fabric of the America of sixties and it is also apparent in the literature of the new generation. In no other quality is this first in men more apparent than in the depth of involvement and identity which is everywhere revealed. The American writers to-day are not aloof from the wishes, the visions and the frustrations of the human being looking for the stars in a world where clouds form on the horizon. Thomas Wolfe was not out of key with the coming generation when he wrote at the end of his life, "The essence of all faith for people of my belief is that man's life can be, and will be better." This belief in the creative power of the human spirit to endure and to prevail whatever the obstacles or the fables of the individual, is still central and fundamental in the literature of America. This expectation, this confident assurance, as expressed by William Faulkner in his speech at Stockholm as he received the Nobel Prize for literature, still sees that though he may never reach them man still grasps for the stars.

American literature starts its journey, in the real sense of the term, with Anne Bradstreet (1612-1672), the first American woman who published a book of poems printed in England followed by Edward Taylor (1644-1729) who wrote *Metrical History of Christianity;* Michael Wigglesworth (1631-1705) wrote *The Day of Doom;* Samuel Sewall (1652-1730) recorded *Diary* which is lively and engaging; Mary Rowlandson (1635-1678) gave a moving account of her eleven-week captivity in 1676; Cotton Mather (1663-1728) wrote *Magnalia Christi Americana;* Roger Williams (1603-1683) wrote *A Key into the Languages of America;* John Woolman (1720-1772) wrote 'Some Considerations on the Keeping of Negroes,' Jonathan Edwards (1703-1758) wrote a sermon, 'Sinners in the Hands of an Angry God;' William Byrd (1674-1744) wrote *History of the Dividing Line;* Robert Beverley (1673-1722) wrote *The History and Present State of Virginia;* Olaudah Equiano (1745-1797) wrote an autobiography, *The Interesting Narrative of the Life of Olaudah or Gustavus Vassa, The African;* Jupiter Hamman (1720-1800) wrote 'An Evening Thought,' the first poem published by a black male in America.

The 18th century American Enlightenment was a movement marked by an emphasis on rationality rather than tradition, scientific inquiry instead of unquestioning religious dogma and representative government in place of monarchy. Enlightenment thinkers and writers were devoted to the ideals of justice, liberty and equality as the natural rights of man. The first enlightenment writer Benjamin Franklin (1706-1790) who wrote *Autobiography* and the second important writer of this group was Hector St. John de Crevecoeur (1735-1813) who wrote *Letters from an American Farmer.* Thomas Paine (1737-1809) wrote *Common Sense* followed by Hartford Wits, Timothy Dwight (1752-1817) wrote *The Conquest of Cannan* based on the story of Joshua's struggle to enter the Promised Land; John Trumbull (1750-1831) wrote *M'Fingal*; Royall Tyler (1757-1826) wrote *The Contrast* and Henry Brakenridge (1748-1816) wrote *Modern Chivalry;* Philip Frenean (1752-1832) edited a number of journals and anthologized 'The Wild Honey Suckle' and Naoh Webster (1758-1843) devised *American Dictionary* and *Spelling Book.* Then came the writers of fiction, Charles Brockden Brown (1771-1810) wrote *Wieland, Arthur Mervyn, Ormond* and *Edgar Huntley;* Washington Irving (1789-1859) wrote *Sketch Book* and *History of New York;* James Fenimore Cooper (1789-1851) wrote *Leather-Stocking* and some women writers as Anne Bradstreet, Anne Hutchinson, Anne Cotton, Phillis Wheatley (1753-1784) wrote poems; Susanna Rowson (1762-1824) wrote *Charlotte Temple;* Hannah Foster (1758-1840) wrote *The Coquette;* Judith Sargent; Murray (1751-1820) wrote under a man's name and Mercy Otis Warren (1728-1814) wrote history of the American Revolution.

Then emerged the transcendalists on the scene. Ralph Waldo Emerson (1803-1882), the towering figure of his era, had a religious sense of mission. He got popularity due to his essays and poems. Henry David Thoreau (1817-1862), the simplest person wrote *Walden* or *Life in the Woods* (1854), Walt Whitman (1819-1892), a self taught who left school at the age of eleven and later wrote *Leaves of Grass* (1855), an epic and as vast energetic and natural as the American continent. His another important work is his long essay *Democratic Vistas* (1871) written during the unrestrained materialism of industrialism's "Gilded Age." Then came the Brahmin Poets and important among them were Henry Wordsworth Longfellow (1807-1882), James Russell Lowell (1819-1891) and Oliver Wendell Holmes (1809-1894). Longfellow wrote 'Evengaline' (1847), 'The Song of Hiawatha (1855) and 'The Courtship of Miles Standish' (1858). Lowell wrote *A Fable for Critics* (1848) and Holmes wrote *The Autocrat of the Breakfast-Table* (1858) and *Elsie Venner* (1861) the two Reformers John Greenleaf Whittier (1807-1892) and Margaret Fuller (1810-1850) emerged before Civil War. Whittier wrote 'Ichabod' and Fuller wrote *Papers on Literature and Art* (1846). Then came Emily Dickinson (1830-1886) who wrote 1,775 poems. She was not widely read but knew the Bible, the works of William Shakespeare and works of classical mythology in great depth.

Walt Whitman, Nathaniel Hawthorne, Herman Melville, Edgar Allan Poe, Emily Dickinson and the transcendalists represent the first great literary generation produced in the United States. In the case of the novelist, the Romantic vision tended to express itself in the form of Hawthorne called the "Romance," a heightened, emotional and symbolic form of the novel. Romances were not the love stories, but serious novels that used special techniques to communicate complex and subtle meanings. Nathaniel Hawthorne (1804-1864) wrote *The Scarlet Letter* (1850) which has become the classic portrayal of Puritan America, *The House of the Seven Gables* (1851) presents the history of New England, *The Bhithedale Romance* (1852) is interesting for its portrait of the socialist, utopian Brook Farm community and his last novel *The Marble Faun* (1860) dwells on the Puritan themes of sin, isolation, expiation and salvation. Herman Melville (1819-1891) wrote *Typee* which was based on his time spent among the supposedly cannibalistic but hospitable tribe of the Taipis in the Marguesas Islands of the South Pacific. *Moby Dick* or *The Whale,* Melville's masterpiece, is the epic story of the whaling ship Peguod and its "ungodly, god like man," Captain Ahab; whose obsessive quest for the white whale Moby Dick leads the ship and its men to destruction. Edgar Allan Poe (1809-1849) shares with Melville a darkly metaphysical vision mixed with elements of realism, parody and burlesque. He refined the short story genre and invented defective fiction. His works include *The Premature Burial, Ligeia, The Cask of Amontillado* and *The Fall of the House of Usher.* His best known poem is *The Raven* (1845).

American women endured many inequalities in the 19th century and they were denied the vote, barred from professional schools and most higher education, forbidden to speak in public and even attend public conventions and unable to own property. Despite these obstacles a strong women's network sprang up. Through letters, personal friendships, formal meetings, women's newspapers and books, women furthered social change. Abolitionist Lydia Child (1802-1880) was a leader of this network and her novel *Hobomok* (1824) shows the need for racial and religious toleration. The first anti-slavery tract, *An Appeal in Favor of that Class of Americans Called Africans* (1833) made her notorious and ruined her financially. Then two sisters Angelina Grimke (1805-1879) and Sarah Grimke (1792-1873) defended the rights of blacks and women. Elizabeth Cady Stanton (1815-1902) wrote *The Woman's Bible* (1895) which discerns a deep-seated anti-female bias in Judaeo-Christian tradition. Sojourner Truth (1797-1883) epitomized the endurance and charisma of this extraordinary group of women. Her life is told in the *Narrative of Sojourner Truth* (1850), an autobiographical account transcribed and edited by Olive Gilbert. Illiterate her whole life, she spoke Dutch-accented English. Harriet Beecher Stowe (1811-1896) wrote *Uncle Tom's Cabin* which was the most popular American book of the 19th century. Forty different publishers printed it in England alone, and it was quickly translated into 20 languages, receiving the praise of such authors as Georges Sand in France, Heinrich Heine in Germany and Ivan Turgenev in Russia. Its passionate appeal for an end to slavery in the United States inflamed the debate that, within a decade, led to the U.S. Civil War (1861-1865). Harriet Jacobs (1818-1896), born a slave, was taught to read and write by her mistress, and on her mistress's death, she was sold to a white master who tried to force her to have sexual relations. Under the pseudonym 'Linda Brent' she wrote her autobiography, *Incidents in the Life of a Slave Girl* (1861) in which she openly condemned the sexual exploitation of black slave women. Harriet Wilson (1807-1870) was the first African-American to publish a novel in the United States—*Our Nig* or Sketches from the Life of a Free Black, in a two storey white house, North, showing that *Slavery's Shadow Fall Even There* (1859). The novel realistically dramatizes the marriage between a white woman and a black man, and also depicts the difficult life of a black servant in a wealthy Christian's house. The most famous black American anti-slavery leader and orator of the era was Frederick Douglass (1817-1895). In 1845, he published *Narrative of the Life of Frederick—An American Slave.* Douglass's narrative is vivid and highly literate and it gives unique insight into the mentality of slavery and the agony that institution caused among blacks.

The U.S. Civil War (1861-1865) between the industrial North and the agricultural slave-owing South was a watershed in American history. As industrialization grew, so did alienation. Characteristic American novels of the period—Stephen Crane's *Maggie: A Girl of the Streets,* Jack London's Martin Eden, and later Theodore Dreiser's *An American Tragedy* depict the damage of economic forces and alienation on the weak and vulnerable individual. Samuel Clemens (1835-1910), better known by his pen name of Mark Twain, grew up in the Mississippi River frontier town of Hannibal, Missouri. Ernest Hemingway's famous statement that all of American literature comes from one great book, Twain's *Adventures of Hucklebury Finn,* indicates this author's towering place in the tradition. *Hucklebury Finn* has countless literary interpretations. The novel is a story of death, rebirth and initiation. The escaped slave, Jim, becomes a father figure for Hick; in deciding to save Jim, Huck grows morally beyond the bounds of his slave-owing society. It is Jim's adventures that initiate Huck into the complexities of human nature and give him moral courage. For many years the editor of the important Atlantic Monthly magazine, William Dean Howells (1837-1920) published realistic local color writing by Bret Harte, Mark Twain, George Washington Cable, and others.

He was the champion of realism, and his novels, such as *A Modern Instance* (1882), *The Rise of Silas Laphan* (1885), and *A Hazard of New Fortunes* (1890), carefully interweave social circumstances with the emotions of middle class Americans. Henry James (1843-1916) wrote that art, especially literary, "makes life, makes interest, makes importance." James's fiction and criticism is the most highly consciousness, sophisticated, and difficult of its era. James is famous for his "international theme"—that is, the complex relationships between native Americans and cosmopolitan Europeans. James's works are *Transatlantic Sketches* (travel pieces, 1875), *The American* (1877), *Daisy Miller* (1879) and a masterpiece, *The Portrait of a Lady* (1881). Like James, Edith Wharton (1862-1937) contrasts American and Europeans. The core of her concern is the gulf separating social reality and the inner self. Wharton had personally experienced such entrapment as a young writer suffering a long nervous breakdown partly due to the conflict in roles between writer and wife. Her best novels include *The House of Mirth* (1905), *The Custom of the Country* (1913), *Summer* (1917) *The Age of Innocence* (1920), and the beautifully, crafted novella *Ethan Frome* (1911). Wharton's and James's dissections of hidden sexual and financial motivations of work link them with writers who seem superficially quite different. Stephen Crane, Jack London, Frank Norris, Theodore Dreiser and Upton Sinclair. Like the cosmopolitan novelists, but much more explicitly, these naturalists used realism to relate the individual to society. Often they exposed social problems and were influenced by Darwinian thought and the related philosophical doctrine of determinism; which views individuals as the helpless pawns of economic and social forces beyond their control. Stephen Crane (1817-1900) wrote many short stories such as "The' Open Boat," "The Blue Hotel" and "The Bride Comes to Yellow Sky." His novel, *The Red Badge of Courage,* was published to great acclaim in 1895; but he barely had time to bask in the attention before he died, at 29, having neglected his health. He was virtually forgotten during the first two decades of the 20th century, but he was resurrected though a laudatory biography by Thomas Beer in 1923. Crane's *Maggie: A Girl of the Street* (1893) is one of the best, if not earliest, naturalistic American novels. It is narrowing story of a poor, sensitive young girl whose uneducated, alcoholic parents utterly fail her. In love and eager to escape her violent home life, she allows herself to be seduced into living with a young man, who soon deserts her when her self-righteous mother rejects her, Maggie becomes a prostitute to survive, but soon commits suicide out of despair. Jack London (1876-1916), a poor self-taught worker from California, the naturalist Jack was catapulted from poverty to fame by his first collection of stories, *The Son of the Wolf* (1900). Other of his best sellers, including *The Call of the Wild* (1903) and *The Sea-Wolf* (1904), made him the highest paid writer in the United States of his time. The autobiographical novel, *Martin Eden* (1909) depicts the inner stresses of the American dream as Jack experienced them during his meteoric rise from obscure poverty to wealth and fame. Theodore Dreiser (1871-1945) in his work *An American Tragedy* (1925) explores the dangers of the American dream. It is a reflection of the dissatisfaction, envy, and despair that afflicted many poor and working people in America's competitive, success driven society.

The great tradition of American investigative journalism had its beginning in this period, during which national magazines such as McClures and Collier's published Ida M. Tarbell's *History of the Standard Oil Company* (1904), Lincoln Stephen's *The Shame of the Cities* (1904); and other hard-hitting exposes, Muckraking novels used eye-catching journalistic techniques to depict harsh working conditions and oppressions. Populist Frank Norris's *The Octopus* (1901) exposed big railroad companies, while socialist Upton Sinclair's *The Jungle* (1906) painted the squator of the Chicago meat-packing houses. By the turn of the century, Chicago had become a great city, home of innovative architecture and cosmopolitan art collections. Chicago was also the home of Harriet Monroe's Poetry, the most important literary magazine of the day. Among the intriguing contemporary poets the journal printed was Edgar Lee Masters (1868-1950), author of the daring, *Spoon River Anthology* (1915), with its new 'unpoetic' colloquial style, frank presentation of sex, critical view of village life, and intensely imagined inner lives of ordinary people. *Spoon River Anthology* is a collection of portraits presented as colloquial epitaphs summing up the lives of individual villagers as if in their own words. It presents a panorama of a country village through its cemetery: 250 people buried there speak, revealing their deepest secrets. Many of the people are related; members of about twenty families speak of their failures and dreams. If in free-verse monologues that are surprisingly modern. Carl Sandburg (1878-1967), a poet, historian, biographer, novelist, musician, essayist, was son of a railroad blacksmith. A journalist by profession, he wrote a massive biography of Abraham Lincoln that is one of the classic works of the 20th century. Vachel Lindsay (1879-1931) was a celebran of small town midwestern populism and creator of strong, rhythmic poetry designed to be declaimed aloud. His work forms a curious link between the popular, or folk, forms of poetry; such as Christian gospel songs and vaude ville (popular theater) on the one hand, and advanced modernist poetics on the other. An extremely popular public reader in his day, Lindsay's prefigure "Beat" poetry readings of the post-World War II era that were accompanied by jazz. Racist by today's standards, his famous poem "The Congo" (1914) celebrates the history of Africans by mingling jazz, poetry, music and chanting. Edwin Arlington Robinson (1869-1935) is the best U.S. poet of the late 19th century. He is famous for short, ironic character studies of ordinary individuals. Robinson's famous dramatic monologues are "Lake Havergal" (1896), about a forsaken lover, "Miniver Cheevy" (1910), a portrait of a romantic dreamer, and "Richard Cory" (1896), a somber portrait of a wealthy man who commits suicide. Then two women novelists Ellen Glasgow (1873-1945) and Willa Cather (1873-1947) explored women's lives placed in brilliantly evoked regional settings. Neither novelist set out to address specifically female issues; their early works usually treat male protagonists, and only as they gained artistic confidence and maturity did they turn to depictions of women's lives. Glasgow and Cather can only be regarded as "Women writers" in a descriptive sense, for their works resist categorisation. Glasgow's *Virginia* (1912) focused on the southern experience, while *Barren Ground* (1925) acknowledged as her best dramatize gifted women attempting to surmount the claustrophic, traditional southern code of domesticity, piety, and dependence for women. Cather immortalized in *O Pioneers!* (1913), *My Antonia* (1918) and her well-known story *Neighbour Rosicky* (1928). Later she became alienated from the materialism of modern Life and wrote of alternative visions in the American Southwest. *Death Comes for the Archbishop* (1927) evokes the idealism of two 16th century priests establishing the Catholic Church in the New Mexican desert. Her works commemorate important aspects of the American experience outside the literary mainstream.

Then we come across the rise of Black American Literature. Booker T. Washington (1856-1915), educator and the most prominent black leader of his day, grew up as a slave in Franklin County, Virginia, born to a white slave-holding father and a slave mother. His autobiography, *Up From Slavery* (1901) recounts his successful struggle to better himself. He became renowned for his efforts to improve the lives of African-Americans; his policy of accommodation with whites—an attempt to involve the recently freed black American in the mainstream of American society—was outlined in his famous *Atlanta Exposition Address* (1895). W.E.B. Du Bois (1868-1963) born in New England and educated at Harvard University wrote "Of Mr. Booker T. Washington and Others," an essay later collected in his landmark book *The Souls of Black Folk* (1903) where he clearly demonstrates that despite his many accomplishments Washington had, in effect, accepted segregation. Like Du Bois, James Weldon Johnson (1871-1938) got inspiration in African-American spirituals which he expressed in his poem "O Black and Unknown Bards" (1917). He further explored the complex issue of race in his fictional *Autobiography of an Ex-Colored Man* (1912) about a mixed-race man who "passes" for white. Charles Waddell Chesnutt (1858-1932), author of two collections of stories, *The Conjure Woman* (1899) and *The Wife of His Youth* (1899), several novels including *The Marrow of Tradition* (1901) was ahead of his time. His stories dwell on racial themes but avoid predictable endings and generalized sentiment.

Several historians have characterized the period between the two world wars as the United States 'traumatic "coming of age," despite the fact that U.S. direct involvement was relatively brief (1917-1918). In the postwar "Big Boom," business flourished, and the successful prospered beyond their wildest dreams. For the first time, many Americans enrolled in higher education—in the 1920s college enrollment doubled. The large cultural wave of Modernism, which gradually emerged in Europe and the United States in the early years of the 20th century, expressed a sense of modern life through art as a sharp break from the past, as well as from Western civilization's classical traditions. In literature, Gertrude Stein (1874-1946) developed an analogue to modern art. By dislocating grammar and punctuation, she achieved new 'abstract' meanings as in her influential collection *Tender Buttons* (1914). Ezra Pound (1885-1972) was one of the most influential American poets of this century. From 1908 to 1920, he resided in London where he associated with many writers, including W.B. Yeats, for whom he worked as a secretary, and T.S. Eliot, whose *Wasteland* he drastically edited and improved. He was a link between the United Stated and Britain, acting as contribution editor to Harriet Monroe's important Chicago Magazine Poetry and spear-heading the new school of poetry known as Imagism. Pound's interests and reading were universal and his life-work was *The Cantos,* which he wrote and published until his death. T.S. Eliot (1888-1965) was born in St. Louis, Missouri, to a well-to-do family and received the best education of any major American writer of his generation at Harvard College, the Sorbonne and Merton College of Oxford University. He studied Sanskrit and Oriental philosophy which influenced his poetry. Like Pound, he went to England and became a towering figure in the literary world. As a critic, Eliot is best remembered for the formulation of the "Objective correlative" which he described in *The Sacred Wood* and as a poet he became immortal by *The Wasteland.* (1922). Besides these he wrote a number of essays and poems and also a few plays. Robert Frost (1874-1963), a charismatic public reader, was renowned for his tours. His poem "Stopping by Woods on a Snowy Evening" (1923) is almost a hypnotic rhyme. Wallace Stevens (1879-1955), educated at Harvard

College and New York' University Law School, practised Law in New York City from 1904 to 1916. On moving to Hartford, Connecticut, to become an insurance executive in 1916, he continued writing poetry. He developed extremely complex ideas of aesthetic order throughout his life in aptly named books such as *Harmonium* (1931), *Ideas of Order* (1935) and *Parts of a World* (1942). Some of the best known poems are "Sunday Morning," "Peter Quinee at the Clavier," "The Emperor of Icecream" and "Thirteen Ways of Looking at a Blackbird." William Carlos Williams (1883-1963) was a practising pediatrician throughout his life; he delivered over 2000 babies and wrote poems on his prescription pads. He was a classmate of Ezra Pound and Hild Doolittle, and his early poetry reveals the influence of Imagism. He championed the use of colloquial speech and his sympathy for working people, children and everyday events made his poetry attractive and accessible. His popular poems are "The Red Wheelbarrow" (1923) and "The Young Housewife" (1917) and an epic *Paterson* (1946-1958—five vols.), celebrates his hometown of Paterson.

Many American poets of stature and genuine vision arose in the years between the World Wars. Robinson Jeffers (1887-1962) lived in California and wrote of the Spanish rancheros and Indians and their mixed traditions. He is best known for his tragic narratives such as *Tamar* (1924), *Roan Stallion* (1925), *The Tower Beyond Tragedy* (1924) and *Medea* (1946). Edward Estlin Cummings (1894-1962) commonly known as e.e. cummings, wrote attractive, innovative verse distinguished for its humor, grace, celebration of love and eroticism. His famous poem "in Just—" (1920) invites the reader to fill in the missing ideas. Hart Crane (1899-1932) was a tormented young poet who committed suicide at the age of 33 by leaping into the sea. His poem, *The Bridge* (1930) was inspired by the Brooklyn Bridge, in which he ambitiously attempted to review the American cultural experience. His other poems are "Voyages" (1923) and "At Melville's Tomb" (1926) whose ending is a suitable epitaph for Crane. Marianne Moore (1887-1972) wrote poems and they are conventional, yet elaborate and subtle in their versification. Langston Hughes (1902-1967), one of many talented poets of the Harlem Renaissance of the 1920s, wrote "The Negro Speaks of Rivers" (1921). This poem suggests that like the great rivers of the world, African culture will endure and deepen.

The American prose between the wars experimented with viewpoint and form and Americans wrote more realistically. The importance of facing reality became a dominant theme in the 1920s and 1930s. F. Scott Fitzgerald (1896-1940) enlisted in the U.S. Army during the World War I and fell in love with a rich and beautiful girl, Telda Sayre who broke off their engagement because he was relatively poor. After he was discharged at war's end, he went to seek his literary fortune in New York City. His first novel, *This Side of Paradise* (1920), became a best seller and at 24 they married. His secure place in American Literature rests primarily on his novel *The Great Gatsby* (1925), a brilliantly written, economically structured story about the American dream of the self-made man. His other works include *Tender Is the Night* (1934) about a young psychiatrist whose life is doomed by his marriage to an unstable woman and *The Beautiful and the Damned* (1922) contained his exploration of the self-destructive extravagance of his times. Both he and his wife were not able to withstand the stresses of fame and success and they squandered their money. Few writers have lived as colourfully as Ernest Hemingway (1899-1961) whose career could have come out of one of his adventurous novels. Born in Illinois, Hemingway spent childhood vacations in Michigan in hunting and fishing trips. He volunteered for an ambulance unit in France during World War I, but was wounded and hospitalized for six months. After the war, as a war correspondent based in Paris, he met expatriate American writers Sherwood Anderson, Ezra Pound, F. Scott Fitzgerald, and Gertrude Stein. After his first novel *The Sun Also Rises* (1926) brought him name and fame, he covered the Spanish Civil War, World War II, and the fighting in China in 1940s. His other popular novels are *A Farewell to Arms* (1929), *For Whom the Bell Tolls* (1940) and *The Old Man and the Sea* (1952). *The Old Man and the Sea,* a short poetic novel about a poor, old fisherman who heroically catches a huge fish devoured by sharks, won him the Pulitzer Prize in 1953; the next year he received the Nobel Prize. Discouraged by a troubled family background, illness, and the belief that he was losing his gift for writing, Hemingway shot himself to death in 1961. William Faulkner (1897-1962), born to an old southern family, was raised in Oxford, Mississippi, where he lived most of his life. Faulkner created an imaginative landscape, Yoknapatawpha County, mentioned in numerous novels. As an innovative writer, he experimented brilliantly with narrative chronology, different points of view and voices. The best of Faulkner's novels include *The Sound and the Fury* (1929) and *As I Lay Dying* (1930), two modernist works experimenting with viewpoint and voice to probe southern families under the stress of losing a family member, *Light in August* (1932), about complex and violent relations between a white woman and a black man; and *Absalom, Absalom!* (1936), perhaps his finest, about the rise of a sell-made-plantation owner and his tragic fall through racial prejudice and a failure to love. He also wrote three novels focusing on the rise of a degenerate family, *The Hamlet* (1940), *The Town* (1957) and *The Mansion* (1959).

Since the 1890s, an undercurrent of social protest had coursed through American literature, welling in the naturalism of Stephen Crane and Theodore Dreiser and in the clear messages of the muckraking novelists. Harry Sinclair Lewis (1885-1951) was born in Sank Centre, Minnesota, and graduated from Yale University. His *Main Street* (1920) satirized monotonous, hypocritical small town life in Gopher Prairie, Minnesota. His incisive presentation of American life and his criticism of American materialism, narrowness, and hypocrisy brought him national and international recognition. In 1926, he was offered and declined a Pulitzer Prize for *Arrowsmith* (1925), a novel tracing a doctor's efforts to maintain his medical ethics amid greed and corruption. In 1930, he became the first American to win the Nobel Prize for Literature. His other works are *Babbitt* (1922), *Elmer Gantry* (1927) and *Cass Timberlane* (1945). John Dos Passos (1896-1970) began as a left-wing radical but moved to the right as he aged. Dos Passos wrote realistically, in line with the doctrine of socialist realism. His best work achieves a scientific objectivism and almost documentary effect. He developed an experimental college technique for the masterwork U.S.A consisting of *The 42nd Parallel* (1930) and

The Big Money (1936). The sprawling collection covers the social history of the United States from 1900 to 1930 and exposes the moral corruption of materialistic American society. John Steinbeck (1902-1968), like Sinclair Lewis, John Steinbeck is held in higher critical esteem outside the United States than in it today, largely because he received the Nobel Prize for Literature in 1963. His best known work is the Pulitzer Prize winning novel *The Grapes of Wrath* (1939), which follows the travails of a poor Okahoma family that loses its form during the depression and travels to California to seek work. Family members suffer conditions of feudal oppression by rich landowners. Other works set in California include *Torlilla Flat* (1935); *Of Mice and Men* (1937), *Cannery Row* (1945) and *East of Eden* (1952).

During the exuberant 1920s, Harlem, the black community situated uptown in New York City, sparkled with passion and creativity. The sounds of its black American Jazz swept the United States by storm. Countee Cullen (1903-1946), a native of Harlem who was briefly married to W.E.B. Du Bois's daughter, wrote accomplished rhymed poetry, in accepted forms, which was much admired by whites. Jean Toomer (1849-1967), like Cullen, an African-American fiction writer and poet, envisioned an American identity that would transcend race. He brilliantly employed poetic traditions of rhyme and meter and did not seek out new "black" forms for his poetry. His major work, *Cane* (1923) is ambitious and innovative. Richard Wright (1908-1960) was born into a poor Mississippi sharecropping family that his father deserted when the boy was five. Wright was the first African-American novelist to reach a general audience, even though he had barely a ninth grade education. His harsh childhood is depicted in one of his best books, his autobiography *Black Boy* (1945). He was influenced by Sherwood, Anderson, Theodore Dreiser and Sinclair Lewis and later by Gertrude Stein and Jean-Paul Sartre. His other works are *Uncle Tom's Children* (1938), a book of short stories, and the powerful and relentless novel *Native Son* (1940), in which Bigger Thomas, an uneducated black youth, mistakenly kills his white employer's daughter, gruesomely burns the body, and murders his black girl friend—fearing she will betray him. Tora Neale Hurston (1903-1960), born in the small town of Etonville, Florida, is one of the lights of the Harlem Renaissance. She first came to New York City at the age of 16—having arrived as a part of a travelling theatrical troupe, a strikingly gifted story teller who captivated her listeners. Her *Mules and Men* (1935) is the most engaging, genuine, and skillfully written book in the field of folklore. Her most important work, *Their Eyes Were Watching God* (1937), is a moving, fresh depiction of a beautiful mulatto woman's maturation and renewed happiness as she moves through three marriages.

From the Civil War into the 20th century, the southern United States had remained a political and economic back water ridden with racism and superstition. Ironically, the most significant 20th century regional literary movement was that of the fugitives—led by poet-critic-theoretician John Crowe Ransom, poet Allen Tate and novelist-poet-essayist Robert Penn Warren. The Fugitives called for a return to the land and to American traditions that could be found in the South. The movement took its name from a literary magazine, *The Fugitive* published from 1922 to 1925 at Vanderbilt University in Nashville, Jennessee, and with which Ransom, Tate, and Warren were all associated. These three major Fugitive writers were also associated with New Criticism, an approach to understanding literature through close readings and attentiveness to formal patterns (of imagery, metaphors, metrics, sounds and symbols) and their suggested meanings. Ransom, leading theorist of the southern renaissance between the wars, published a book, *The New Criticism* (1941) on this method, which offered an alternative to previous extra-literary methods of criticism based on history and biography. New Criticism became the dominant American critical approach in the 1940s and 1950s.

In 20th century American drama imitated English and European theater. Often, plays from England or translated from Europeans languages dominated theater seasons. But Eugene O'Neill (1888-1953) emerged as a great figure of American Theatre. His plays combine enormous technical originality with freshness of vision and emotional depth. His earlier dramas concern the working class and poor, later works explore subjective realms, such as obsessions and sex, and underscore his reading in Freud and his anguished attempt to come to terms with his dead mother, father and brother. His play *Desire Under the Elms* (1924) recreates the passion hidden within the family; *The Great God Brown* (1926) uncovers the unconsciousness of a wealthy businessman; and *Strange Interlude* (1928), a winner of the Pulitzer Prize, traces the tangled loves of one woman. His later plays include the acknowledged masterpieces *The Iceman Cometh* (1946), a stark work on the theme of death, and *Long Day's Journey Into Night* (1956), a powerful, extended autobiography in dramatic form focusing on his own family. In 1936 he received the Nobel Prize for Literature—the first American playwright to be honored. Thornton Wilder (1897-1975) is known for his plays *Our Town* (1938) and *The Skin of Our Teeth* (1942) and for his novel *The Bridge of San Luis Rey* (1927). *Our Town* conveys positive American values. Clifford Odets (1906-1963), a master of social drama, came from an Eastern European, Jewish immigrant background. His best known play was *Waiting for Lefty* (1935), an experimental one-act drama that fervently advocated labor unionism. His *Awake and Sing*!, a nostalgic family drama, became another popular success, followed by *Golden Boy*, the story of an Italian immigrant youth who ruins his musical talent (a violinist) when he is reduced by the lure of money to become a boxer and injures his hands.

A shift away from an assumption that traditional forms, ideas, and history can provide meaning and continuity to human life has occurred in the contemporary literary imagination throughout many parts of the world, including the United States. Many poets including Brooks, Adrienne Rich, Richard Wilbur, Robert Lowell, and Robert Penn Warren began writing traditionally, using rhyme and metres, but abandoned these in the 1960s under the pressure of public events and a gradual trend toward open forms. Robert Lowell (1917-1977) began traditionally but was influenced by experimental currents. His early books, *Land of Unlikeness* (1944) and *Lord Weary's Castle*

(1946), which won a Pulitzer Prize, revealed great control of traditional forms and styles, strong feeling, and an intensely personal yet historical vision. His next book, *The Mills of the Kavanaughs* (1951), contains moving dramatic monologues in which members of his family reveal their tenderness and failings. Sylvia Plath (1932-1963) lived an outwardly exemplary life, attending Smith College on scholarship, graduating first in her class, and winning a Fulbright grant to Cambridge University in England. There she met her charismatic husband-to-be, poet Ted Hughes, with whom she had two children and settled in a country house in England. Beneath the fairy-tale success festered unresolved psychological problems evoked in her highly readable novel *The Bell Jar* (1963). Some of these problems were personal, while others arose from repressive 1950s attitudes towards women. Plath's storybook life crumbled when she and Hughes separated and she cared for the young children in a London apartment during a winter of extreme cold. Ill, isolated and in despair Plath worked against the clock to produce a series of stunning poems before she committed suicide by gassing herself in her kitchen. These poems were collected in the volume *Ariel* (1965) and Robert Lowell noted in the introduction her poetry's rapid development. Her early poetry is well-crafted and traditional, but her late poems exhibit a desperate bravura and proto-feminist cry of anguish. Anne Sexton (1928-1974) was a passionate woman who attempted to be wife, mother, and poet. Like Plath, she suffered from mental illness, and ultimately committed suicide. Her confessional poetry is more autobiographical than Plath's. Her works include *To Bedlam and Part Way Back* (1960), *Live or Die* (1966) and the posthumous book *The Awful Rowing Toward God* (1975). John Berryman (1914-1972) was educated in Columbia University and later was a fellow at Princeton University. Specializing in traditional forms and metres, he was inspired by early American history and wrote self-critical, confessional poems in his *Dream Songs* (1969). Theodore Roethke (1908-1963) evolved a special language evoking the "greenhouse world." His love poems in *Words for the Wind* (1958) celebrate beauty and desire with innocent passion. Richard Hugo (1923-1982) a native of Seattle, Washington, studied under Theodore Roethke and grew up poor in dismal urban environments. Hugo wrote nostalgic, confessional poems in bold iambics about shabby, forgotten small towns in his part of the United States. Philip Levine, born in 1928, deals directly with the economic sufferings of workers through keen observation, rage and painful irony. In terms of his rhythmic pattern, he has travelled in path from traditional metres in his early works to a freer, more open line in his later poetry as he expresses his lonely protest against the evils of the contemporary world. James Dickey, born in 1923, a novelist and essayist as well as poet, is a native of Georgia. Much of his writings is rooted in nature—rivers and mountains, weather patterns and the perils lurking within. In the later 1960s he wrote a novel, *Deliverance,* about the dark side of male bonding, which, when published and later filmed, increased his renown. His collections of verse deal with such varied themes as the landscape of the South, Jericho, The South Beheld (1974) and the influence of the Bible on his life, God's Images (1977). Elizabeth Bishop (1911-1979) and Andrienne Rich, born in 1929, have garnered much respect among women poets in recent past. Bishops's crystalline intelligence and interest in remote landscapes and metaphors of travel appeal to readers for their exactitude and society. Bishop may be placed in a "Cool" female poetic tradition harking back to Emily Dickinson, in comparison with the "hot" poems of Plath, Sexton, and Adrienne Rich. Though Adrienne began by writing poems in traditional form and metre, her works, particularly those written after she became an ardent feminist in the 1960s, embody strong emotions. Her special genius in the metaphor, as in her extraordinary work, "Diving Into the Wreck" (1973), evoking a woman's search for identity in terms of diving down to a wrecked ship. Her other poem "The Roofwalker" (1961) is dedicated to poet Denise Leverto.

Lowell's mature achievement and much of contemporary poetry lies in the experimentation begun in the 1950s by a number of poets. This may be divided into five loose schools, identified by Donald Allen in his *The New American Poetry* (1960), the first anthology to present the work of those poets who were previously neglected by the critical and academic communities. The first school known as The Black Mountain School centred around Black Mountain College, an experimental liberal arts college in Asheville, North Carolina, where poets Charles Olson, Robert Duncan and Robert Creely taught in the early 1950s. Ed Dorn, Joel Oppenheimer, and Jonathan Williams studied there, and Paul Blackburn, Larry Eigner, and Denise Levertov published work in the school's magazines, *Origin* and the *Black Mountain Review.* The second school known as The San Francisco School includes most West Coast poetry in general and owes much to Eastern philosophy and religion, as well as to Japanese and Chinese poetry. San Francisco poets include Jack Spicer, Lawrence Ferlinghetti, Robert Duncan, Phil Whalen, Lew Welch, Gary Snyder, Kenneth Rexroth, Joanne Kyger, and Diane de Prima. Their poetry is often simple accessible and optimistic. The Third group known as Beat Poets emerged in the 1950s. Most of the important Beat Poets migrated to San Francisco from the East Coast and these include Allen Glinsberg, Gregory Corso, Jack Kerouac, and William Burroughs. Beat Poetry is oral, repetitive, and immensely effective in readings, largely because it developed out of poetry readings in underground clubs. The fourth school known as The New York School are not interested in overtly moral questions, and, in general they steer clear of political issues. They have the best education and they are John Ashbey, Frank O'Hara, and Kenneth Koch. Their poems are fast moving, full of urban detail, incongruity, and an almost palpable sense of suspended belief. The fifth group has no clear geographical underpinning. This agree group includes recent movements and experiments. Chief among these are surrealism, which expresses the unconsciousness through vivid, dream like imagery, and much poetry by women and ethnic minorities that has flourished in recent past. Superficially distinct, surrealists, feminists, and minorities appear to share a sense of alienation from white, male, mainstream literature. Although Eliot, Stevens and Pound had introduced symbolist techniques into American poetry in the 1920s, surrealism, the major force in European poetry and thought in Europe during and after World War II, did not take root in the United States. During the 1960s, many American Writers—W.S. Merwin, Robert Bly, Charles Simic, and Mark

Strand, among others—turned to French and especially Spanish Surrealism for its pure emotion, its archetypal images, and its models of anti-rational, existential unrest.

Women's literature, like minority literature and surrealism, first became aware of itself as a driving force in American Life during the late 1960s. It flourished in the feminist movement initiated in the era. Distinguished women poets include Amy Clampitt, Rita Dove, Louise Gluck, Jorie Graham, Carolyn Kizer, Maxine Kumin, Denise Levertov, Andre Lorde, Gjertrud Schnackenberg, May Swenson, and Mona Van Duyn.

The second half of the 20th century has witnessed a renaissance in multiethnic literature. Beginning with the 1960s, following the lead of African-Americans, ethnic writers in the United States began to command public attention. During the 1970s, ethnic studies programs were begun. In the 1980s, a number of academic journals, professional organizations, and literary magazines devoted to ethnic groups were initiated. By the 1990s, conferences devoted to the study of specific ethnic literature had begun and the canon of "classics" had been expanded to include ethnic writers in anthologies and course lists. Important issues include race versus ethnicity, ethnocentrism versus polycentrism, monolingualism versus bilingualism and coaption versus marginalization. Minority poetry shares the variety and occasionally the anger of women's writing. It has flowered recently in Hispanic-Americans such as Gray Soto, Alberto Rios, and Lorna Dee Cervantes; in native Americans such as Leslie Marmon Silko, Simon Ortiz and Louise Endrich; in African-American writers such as Amiri Baraka, Michael Harper, Rita Dove, Maya Angelou, and Nikki Giovanni, and in Asian-American poets such as Cathy Song, Lawson Inada and Janice Mirikitani.

Recent directions in American poetry include the language poets loosely associated with *Temblor* magazine. Among them are Bruce Andrews, Lyn Hejinian, Douglas Messerli (editor of 'Language' Poetries: An Anthology (1987)], Bob Perelman, and Barret Watten, author of *Total Syntax* (1985), a collection of essays. They stretch language to reveal its potential for ambiguity, fragmentation, and self assertion with chaos.

The late 1940s saw the aftermath of World War II as well as the flourishing of a new contingent of writers. They explored the fate of the individual within the family or community and focused on the balance between personal growth and responsibility to the group. Robert Penn Warren (1905-1989), one of the Southern Fugitives enjoyed a fruitful career running through most of the 20th century. He showed a lifelong concern with democratic values as they appeared within historical context. The most enduring of his novels is *All the King's Men* (1946), focusing on the darker implications of the American dream. Arthur Miller, born in 1945, dramatist-novelist-essayist-biographer, reached his personal pinnacle in 1949 with *Death of a Salesman,* a study of man's search for merit and worth in his life and the realization that failure invariably looms. His other works are *All My Sons* (1947) and *The Crucible* (1953). Tennessee Williams (1911-1983), a native of Mississippi, was one of the more complex individuals on the American literary scene of the mid-20th century. His work focused on disturbed emotions and unresolved sexuality within families. He wrote more than twenty dramas, many of them autobiographical. He reached his peak relatively early in his career, in the 1940s, with *The Glass Managerie* (1944) and *A Street Car Named Desire* (1947), Katherine Anne Porter (1890-1980) had a long life and career. Her story collections include *Flowering Judas* (1930), *Noon Wine* (1937), *Pale Horse, Pale Rider* (1939), *The Leaning Tower* (1944) and *Collected Stories* (1965). Eudora Welty, born in 1909, was guided by Warren and Porter. Despite violence in her work, Welty's wit is essentially humane and affirmative. Her collections of stories include *The Wide Net* (1943), *The Golden Apples* (1949), *The Bride of Innisfallen* (1955), and *Moon Lake* (1980). He has also written novels such as *Delta Wedding* (1946) and *The Optimists' Daughter* (1972).

The 1950s saw the delayed impact of modernization and technology in everyday life, left over the 1920s before the Great Depression, and the 1950s provided most Americans with time to enjoy long awaited material prosperity. The 1950s actually was a decade of subtle and pervasive stress. Novels of John O'Hara, John Cheever and John Updike explore the stress lurking in the shadows of seeking satisfaction. John O'Hara (1905-1970), trained as journalist, was a prolific writer of plays, stories and novels. His famous works are *Appointment in Samarra* (1934), *Ten North Frederick* (1955) and *From the Terrace* (1958). James Baldwin (1924-1987) argued for an end to separation between the races. His works include *Go Tell It On the Mountain* (1953), *Another Country* (1962) and *Nobody Knows My Name* (1961). Ralph Waldo Ellison (1914-1994) had one of the strangest careers in American Letters consisting of one highly acclaimed book, *Invisible Man* (1952) and nothing more. It embodies a powerful racial theme because the "invisible man" is invisible not in himself but because others, blinded by prejudice cannot see him for who he is. Flannery O'Connor (1925-1964) a native of Georgea, lived a life cut short by lupus, a deadly blood disease. Still, he refused sentimentality, as evident in her extremely humorous yet bleak and uncompromising stories. Her works include short story collections *A Good Man Is Hard to Find* (1955) and *Everything That Rises Must Converge* (1965); the novel *The Violent Bear It Away* (1960); and a volume of letters, *The Habit of Being* (1979). Saul Bellow, born in 1915 in Canada and raised in Chicago, is of Russian-Jewish background. He studied anthropology and sociology, which greatly influenced his writing. He received Nobel Prize for Literature in 1976. His works include *Dangling Man* (1944), *The Victim* (1947), *The Adventures of Augie March* (1953), *Seize the Day* (1956), *Henderson the Rain King, Herzog* (1964), *Mr. Sammler's Planet* (1970), *Humboldt's Gift* (1975), *The Dean December* (1982) and *A Theft* (1989). Bernard Malamud (1914-1986) was born in New York City to Russian-Jewish immigrant parents. He was awarded the Pulitzer Prize and National Book Award. His works include *The Assistant* (1957), *The Natural* (1952), *A New Life* (1961), *The Fixer* (1966), *Pictures of Fidelmen* (1969) and *The Tenants* (1971). His stories in collection include *The Magic Barrel* (1958), *Idiots First* (1963) and *Rembrandt's Hat* (1973). He conveyed a sense of Jewish present and past, the real and the surreal, fact and legend. Isaac Bashevis Singer (1904-1991), a native of Poland who immigrated to the United States in 1935, was Nobel Prize-winning novelist and short story writer. His works include *The Monor* (1967) and *The Estate.* (1969), set in the 19th century

Russia, and *The Family Moskat* (1950), focused on a Polish-Jewish family between the World Wars. Vladimir Nabokov (1889-1977) was an Eastern European immigrant. His works include *Pnin* (1957), about an intellectual Russian emigre' professor, *Lolita* (1958), about an educated, middle aged European who becomes infatuated with an ignorant 12-year old American girl and *Pale Fire* (1962), focus on a long poem by an imaginary dead poet and the commentaries on it by a critic whose writings overwhelm the poem and take on unexpected lives of their own. John Cheever (1912-1982) is known for his elegant, suggestive short stories and called a 'novelist of manners.' His stories include 'The Way Some People Live' (1943). 'The Housebreaker of Shady Hill' (1958), 'Some People, Places and Things That Will Not Appear in My Next Novel' (1961), 'The Brigadier and The Golf Widow' (1964), and 'The World of Apples' (1973). His novels are *The Wapshot Scandal* (1964), *Bullet Park* (1969), and *Falconer* (1977). John Updike, born in 1932, is best known for his four Rabbit books: *Rabbit, Run* (1960), *Rabbit Redux* (1971), *Rabbit Is Rich* (1981) and *Rabbit at Rest* (1990). His other novels are *The Centaur* (1963), *Couples* (1968), and *Bech: A Book* (1970). He also wrote short stories which include 'The Same Door' (1959), 'The Music School' (1966), 'Museums and Women' (1972), 'Too Far to Go' (1979), and 'Problems' (1979). J.D. Salinger, born in 1919, became a popular novelist with the publication of his novel *The Catcher in the Rye* (1951). His other works include *Nine Stories* (1953), *Franny and Looey* (1961) and *Raise High the Roof-Beam Carpenters* (1963). Jack Kerouac's (1922-1969) fictional work was much influenced by Southern novelists. His works include *On the Road* (1957), *The Dharma Bums* (1958), and *Mexico City Blues* (1959).

The alienation and stress underlying the 1950s found outward expression in the 1960s in the United States in The Civil Rights Movement, feminism, antiwar protests, minority activitism, and the arrival of a counter-culture whose effects are still being worked through American society. Notable political social works of the era include the speeches of civil rights leader Dr. Martin Luther King, Jr., the early writings of feminist leader Betty Friedan (*The Feminist Mystique,* 1963) and Norman

Mailer's *The Armies of the Night* (1968), about a 1967 antiwar march. Turmon Capote wrote *Breakfast at Tiffiny's* (1958) and *In Cold Blood* (1966). At that time the "New Journalism" emerged and volumes of non-fiction that combined journalism with techniques of fiction to add to the drama and immediacy of the story being reported. Tom Wolfe wrote the *Electric Kool-Aid Acid Test* (1968), *The Right Stuff* (1979), and a novel, *The Bonfire of the Vanities* (1987). Walker Percy, a physician by training, wrote *The Moviegoer* (1961) and *The Last Gentleman* (1966). Thomas Pychon, born in 1937, wrote *V* (1963), *The Crying of Lot 49* (1966) and *Gravity's Rainbow* (1973). John Barth, born in 1930, wrote *The Floating Opera* (1956), *Giles Goat-Boy* (1966), *The End of the Road* (1958) *The Sot-Weed Factor* (1960), Chimera (1972); *Letters* (1979) and *Sabbatical: A Romance* (1982). Norman Mailer, born in 1923, wrote *Miami and the Siege of Chicago* (1968), *The Executioner's Song* (1979), *Ancient Evenings* (1983) and *Harlots' Ghost* (1992).

By the mid-1970s, an era of consolidation began and the Vietnam conflict was over followed by U.S. recognition of the People's Republic of China and America's Bicentennial celebration. The 1980s, the "*Me Decade,*" ensued in which individuals tended to focus more on personal concerns than on larger social issues. John Gardner (1933-1982), from a farming background, was a professor of English and wrote *Grendel* (1971), *The Resurrection* (1966), *The Sunlight Dialogues* (1972), *Nickel Mountain* (1973), *October Light* (1976) and *Mickon's Ghost* (1982). Toni Morrison, born in 1931, worked as a distinguished professor at various universities and wrote *The Bluest Eye* (1970), Sula (1973), Song of Solomon (1977), *Tar Baby* (1981), *Beloved* (1987). Morrison won the Nobel Prize for Literature in 1993. Alice Walker, an African-American born in 1944, wrote *The Color Purple.* It is the story of the love between two poor black sisters that survives a separation over years. It recalls Maya Angelon's *I Know Why the Caged Bird Sings* (1970).

Minority writing became a major fixture on the American Literary scene between 1980 and 1990. August Wilson's *Fences* (1986) and *The Piano Lesson* (1989) brought the Pulitzer Prize. David Henry Hwang, a California born son of Chinese immigrants, made his mark in drama with his plays such as *F.O.B.* (1981) and M. Butterfly (1986). A new group on the literary scene were the Hispanic-American writers, including the Pulitzer Prize-winning novelist Oscar Hijuelos, the Cuban born author of *The Mambo Kings Play Songs of Love* (1989), short story writer Sandra Cisneros who wrote *Women Hollering Creek and Other Stories* (1991) and Rudolfo Anaya wrote *Bless Me Ultima* (1972). For sometime regionalism has been making a return in American literature enabling readers to get a sense of time and humanity and it is evident from novels, short stories and drama written in the decade. In his regard we may refer to William Kennedy's *Ironweed* (1983) and *Very Old Bones* (1992) which show the lives of the denizens of the streets and saloons of the New York State Capital city; Carol Oate's *The Wheel of Love* (1970) and *Where Are You Going, Where Have You Been?* (1974) are her best works. Anne Tyler's *Dinner at the Homesick Restaurant* (1982), *The Accidental Tourist* (1985), *Breathing Lessons* (1988), and *Saint May be* (1991) brought good name and fame to her in literary field. *Ward Justs', a former international correspondent, Nicholson at Large* (1975), *In the City of Fear* (1982) and *Jack Gance* (1989) are his impressive works. Reynolds Price became popular with his novel *A Long and Happy Life* (1962), *Kate Vaiden* (1986) and *Blue Colhoun* (1992). McCorkle wrote *The Cheer Leader* (1984), *Tending to Virginia* (1987) and *Crash Diet* (1992). Pat Conroy came out with *The Great Santini* (1976) and *The Prince of Tides* (1986). Jane Smiley won Pulitzer Prize in 1992 for *A Thousand Acres* (1991) resembles Shakespeare's *King Lear.* Larry McMurty wrote *Lonesome Dove* (1985), *Anything For Billy* (1988) and *The Last Picture.* Cormac McCarthy, considered heir to the southern Gothic tradition, wrote *Blood Meridian* (1985), *All The Pretty Horses* (1992) and *The Crossing* (1994). Leslie Marmon Silko's *Ceremony* (1977) made her popular. N. Scott Momaday's *The Way to Rainy Mountain* brought good name to him. James Welch described the struggles of Native Americans in *Winter in the Blood* (1974), *The Death of Jim Loney* (1979), *Fools Crow* (1986) and *The Indian Lawyer* (1990). Thomas McGuane wrote *Ninety-Two in The Shade* (1973) and *Keep the Change* (1989). Louise Erdrich's *Love Medicine* (1984) presents a blend of stoicism and humour. Wallace Stegner wrote *The Big Rock Candy Mountain* (1943) and *Angle of Repose* for which he won 1971 Pulitzer Prize. Joan Didion a journalist and a novelist, wrote *Slouching Tward Bethlehem* and *Play It As It Lays* (1970). Raymond Carver wrote *What We Talk About When We Talk About Love* (1977) and *Where I'm Calling From* (1986) in which he placed the working class against the backdrop of their scenic surroundings.

Thus, we find that American literature has traversed an extended, winding path from pre-colonial days to contemporary times. Society, history, technology all have had telling impact on it. Ultimately, though, there is a constant—humanity, with all its radiance and its malevolence, its tradition and its promise.

2

American Women's Drama and Its Critics

VERA SHAMINA

Nowadays nobody argues any more that women's drama, both in America and in Europe, has become a relevant part of contemporary theatre. Apart from the plays themselves written by talented women-playwrights there appeared many critical essays and monographs devoted to feminist theatre which made considerable contribution to the process of acknowledgement and understanding of women's drama as a valuable artistic phenomenon. Among those in the US are such authoritative critics as Rudy Cohn, Helen Keissar, Janet Brown, Mary Dale, Elizabeth Natalle, Yvonne Shafer and some others. In their works they have presented a comprehensive picture of modern women's drama, tracing it back to its sources in the nineteenth and the first half of the twentieth century. Not questioning the value and significance of their critical analysis I would like to argue some points which seem relevant to clarify when studying women's theatre.

First and foremost it concerns terminology. Some critics call everything written by women "feminist" while others refer this term only to the plays with specifically feminist message and certain stage technique. Honor Moore, for example, suggests that any play is a feminist drama "if a woman can identify with its characters and situations" (Brown 70). This approach is shared by Linda Killian who defines feminist drama as "something written by women, which tries to explore the female psyche, women's place in society, women's potential" (Natalle 25). It is obvious that such definitions are very vague and tell very little if anything about the specific nature of feminist theatre, they also do not reflect its innovative character that is often stressed by feminist critics. I personally side with those who define as "feminist" only such plays in which the issues of feminist ideology are brought to the foreground and totally determine their subject-matter. Though we find here great variety of opinions, all of them tend to look for particular characteristics of feminist drama, which enable to define it as a special artistic phenomenon. Thus,, an authoritative theatre critic Helen Keissar, the author of the monograph "Feminist Theatre" calls feminist drama "distinct theatrical genre," which came into being in 1960s (Keissar 2), which in her opinion asserts a new aesthetic based on "the transformation" as opposed to the old one based on "recognition" (Keissar 2). Transformation in this case is understood as emancipation from "the stereotyped gender roles," imposed by the society (Keissar 68). As an example, the critic gives the play by Mirna Lamb "But what have you done for me lately," which the scholar views as "a paradigm for the feminist theatre" (Keissar 104). It shows a pregnant man who comes to a woman doctor pleading her for an abortion.

Such cases in which men are shown in the situation traditionally typical for women are quite frequent in modern feminist dramas. But it will be only just to mention that the trick itself has not been invented by women and is known from the times of Shakespeare and Fielding.

Janet Brown defines feminist drama through the notion of "rhetorical motive," borrowed from Kenneth Burke. She states: "When women's struggle for autonomy is a play's central rhetorical motive that play can be called a feminist drama" (Brown 1). And further on: "If the agent is a woman, her purpose is autonomy and the scene is an unjust socio-sexual hierarchy, the play is a feminist drama" (Brown 22).

Another prominent scholar of feminist theatre,—Elizabeth Natalle also grounds her definition on the principles of rhetoric which she understands as a "persuasive message designed to influence the beliefs and convictions" (Natalle 5). She justly points out that most of the plays created by feminist theatre groups are "message oriented"—"the emphasis is on moral instruction of an audience" (Natalle 32). Probably not realising it herself, when defining the "rhetoric motive" of these plays, she gives them rather an unattractive characteristic: "The main rhetoric of many feminist plays is rejection of male power politics in favour of a society that is characterised by either androgynous or matriarchal traits" (Natalle 38). Thus, one kind of chauvinism is replaced for another.

In my viewpoint, the most distinct and accurate definition of feminist drama is given by Dinah Levitt, who points out the following essential characteristics:

(1) Feminist drama and art are political and associated with women's movement.
(2) The emergent status of feminist theatre accounts for its variety in subject and its visionary point of view.
(3) Feminist drama arrives at the universal through personal.
(4) Feminist theatre is pro-woman.
(5) Feminist theatre is didactic.
(6) Common characteristics of feminist theatre groups—collective organisation (Natalle 4).

Though many of the aforementioned characteristics are quite acceptable, many of them can be easily attributed equally to some of male as well as female dramas. Here we come across the most crucial question: should we at all subdivide literature in general and drama in particular into male and female unless we prove that there is some drastic difference? This concerns American drama criticism where most of the feminist critics view women's drama as an alternative to the mainstream. They claim that the fact that on Broadway as well as in some other influential theatres the plays by women-playwrights for a long time were very scarce can be accounted for only by discrimination against women. The one who strongly objects to that is Lilian Hellman, who to the question on the obstacles she might have faced as a woman-writer for the stage answered: "Listen, I don't write with my genitals.... Let me tell you one thing, the New York theatre is so hard up for good plays,—they'll take it from anywhere they can get it" (Brater ix). Another thing, which should be taken into consideration here, is the criterion, which for a long time determined the choice plays on Broadway. Indeed, in the 1960s-1970s many women-playwrights had to overcome obstacles on their way to the stage. But though this was the period when male chauvinism did play a significant role in American society, the plays of such women-authors just as the plays by Albee, Kopit, Gelber and some other male playwrights were not staged mainly because they offered new, innovative forms and techniques, new ideas which did not fit into the framework of the establishment, no matter who they were introduced by—men or women. It was then that the movement of off-and later off-off-Broadway theatres started, which staged many of the now well-known women-dramatists. This situation however is not true for the present which is definitely due to the collective efforts of American women. One of the few women-critics who does not oppose women's drama to the "male" mainstream but tries to view it in the context of general tendencies of development of American theatre is Ruby Cohn. She even ventures to make such an "anti-feminist" comment as to state that some of contemporary women-dramatists "have yet to match the depth and range of such male colleagues as David Rabe, David Mamet, Sam Shepard" (Cohn 58). Nowadays Broadway is functioning according to rather a strictly observed principle of political correctness, which often makes it easier to stage a weak play written by a woman than a good play written by a man. Thus we perceive here a principle which is very well-known in Russia—the principle of the so-called "social order" when the decisive factor in favour or against a work of art is ideological rather than aesthetic.

This brings us close to the next aspect of feminist criticism that I would like to comment on, that is the analysis of the plays as such.

The absolute majority of the aforementioned critics analyse women's drama from the viewpoint of its rhetoric, practically totally excluding the level of poetic. In my opinion, it is almost impossible to speak about a specific female world-view when we take into consideration only the play's ideological message. Moreover, many of the traits that are given as specific for feminist drama can be easily traced in the works of men-playwrights as well. Thus Helen Keissar speaking about Megan Terry as one of the most characteristic representatives of feminist drama writes: "Megan Terry's dramas unabashedly question the American dream and its corruption in the hands of the greedy and mendacious" (Keissar 70). These words can be referred to the whole of the serious XX-th century American drama.

Karlyn Kohns Campbell finds feminist rhetoric unique in its existence as "a process of discovery a new identity" (Brown 11). Her idea is supported by Gerda Lerner who calls it "the search of autonomy" (Lerner iii). This is actually very similar to what is termed as the search for "belonging," the theme, which was introduced by O'Neill, and since then remained one of the key themes of American drama, both male and female. And Diane Hope in her work "A Rhetorical Definition of Movements" analyses the rhetoric of feminist drama on the basis of death and rebirth pattern (Hope 7), the pattern which, as commonly known, underlies drama as such. The feature that Dinah Leavitt claims to be specific for feminist drama—that is "arriving at the universal through personal" (Natalle 5)—is also common for all "good" dramas. Here, again, we can refer to O'Neill, who declared that he was not interested in the relations of man with man, but only in the relations of man with God.

But still I think that there is a certain female vision of the world, which is implicitly reflected in the poetic of women's drama. It can be traced through the analysis of recurrent images and symbols, key motifs, specific metaphors. Thus, even from a brief overview we can notice that one of the recurrent artistic details in women's dramas is the hair of the main character, the change it undergoes in the course of action. Another image that is often used by women-playwrights is the image of a flowering tree or plant. These images, though not specifically feminist taken together contribute to the peculiar poetic of women's drama. One of the important motifs often met in these plays is the motive of food, meals—the process of cooking and consuming food. We often come across the image of kitchen, which acquires symbolic meaning. Much attention is paid to everyday details, domestic "trifles," as in the eponymous play by Susan Glaspell. In the dramas with distinct feminist rhetoric, such recurrent motifs are the motif of rape, and the motif of sports competition. These are just a few examples, the number of which can be considerably increased.

One of the recurrent passages in feminist criticism is the accusation of male authors of simplifying women-characters, showing them rather as stereotypes than full-blooded images. Though this accusation can also be argued on the examples of many prominent plays written by men-playwrights, I rather suggest reviewing women's drama to find out how male characters are represented. Even from brief overview we can't fail to notice that in the plays with distinctly articulated feminist rhetoric, the characters of men are far from being very deep or psychologically developed. On the average, they can be grouped into the following types: a man with traditional view of gender roles in society, preaching the most primitive ideas about the role of woman in family and society/usually a husband or a boss/a rapist/ the theme of sexual harassment is one of key-themes in feminist dramas/and a misfit, a marginal figure/ usually due to his sexual orientation/who the female protagonist because of that sympathises with. The first two types represent the social system, which is rejected by feminists, and therefore are treated ruthlessly. This can be seen not only from the plays themselves but from the feminist critique as well. Thus Helen Keissar points out that in the plays by Rosalin Drexler whom she considers to be one of the leading representatives of feminist drama, "man is an enemy more starkly and unremittingly than in some other feminist dramas" (Keissar 119). The same critic when giving examples of different forms "forms of theatrical vision of women" during the second wave of feminist drama in the 1970s states: "Beth Henley's 'Crimes of the Heart' encourages the audience to be hostile towards men, but leaves little alternative—for men or for women—other than to shoot any male who displays chauvinistic tendencies" (Keissar 157). In reference to this we may say that men in many of feminist dramas become a kind of scapegoats sacrificed for the sake of a "new woman" who rather ruthlessly establishes her new identity, very often simply killing the man. See, for example, "The Verge" Susan Glaspell, "Machinal" Sophie Tredwell. Diane Hope treats this issue a bit milder. She writes: "Though men are clearly seen as enemies, but men are not victims. The victim is 'traditional woman,' for it is 'the male identified woman' who has been identified as an appendage to man" (Hope 160). Elizabeth Natalle explains it in the following way: "Feminist playwrights deliberately portray characters as opposites. The man exhibits negative traits which arouse animosity of the women towards these characters" (Natalle 52). Thus feminist critics oppose "female" drama to "male" drama mainly because the latter shows "male identified woman" unlike "woman identified woman" in feminist dramas. But here, too, we can argue that the most subtle analysis of a male myth of a 'male identified woman' is given in a play written by a man-playwright—'M. Butterfly' by H.D. Hwang. All this testifies to the fact that a genuine artist is not directly dependent on his or her gender. At the same time, a look of a male or a female at oneself can be equally biased as a look at the opposite sex from aside. That is why, in my opinion instead of opposing women's drama to the mainstream, a critic should look for the points of correlation and interaction, considering the process of drama and theatre development in the U.S. as well as in other countries as heterogeneous. No wonder, many of the prominent women-playwrights object to being labelled as feminist writers.

One of the most distinguished representatives of American drama criticism Robert Brustein wrote on Marsha Norman: "An authentic universal playwright—not a woman playwright, mind you, not a regional playwright, not an ethnic playwright, but one who speaks to the concerns of all mankind" (Shafer 324). These words can be justly referred to the works of all major American women-playwrights, whose creative activity being part and parcel of contemporary theatre process by far surpasses the rigid framework of feminism which some critics tend to restrict them to.

WORKS CITED

Brown, J. *Feminist Drama: Definition and Critical Analysis.* The Scarecrow Press INC. New York @ London: Methuen, 1979.

Cohn, R. *New American Drama*, 1960-1990. Macmillan Education Ltd., 1991.

Enoch. B. (ed.) *Feminist Focus.* New York, Oxford: OUP, 1989.

Hope, D. *A Rhetorical Definition of Movements.* State Univ. of New York at Buffalo, 1975.

Keissar, H. *Feminist Theatre.* Macmillan Publ. Ltd., 1985.

Lerner, G. *The Female Experience.* Indianapolis: Bobbs-Meril Company Inc., 1977.

Natalle, E. *Feminist Theatre: A Study in Persuasion.* The Scarecrow Press INC. New York @ London: Methuen, 1985.

Shafer, I. *American Women Playwrights, 1900-1950.* New York: Peter Lang Publishing Inc., 1975.

3

The Return of the Native American: The Theme of Homecoming in Contemporary Native North American Fiction[1]

MARK SHACKLETON

> "Home is the place where, when you have to go there,
> They have to take you in"
> Robert Frost "The Death of the Hired Man"
> "Home's the place we head for in our sleep"
> Louise Erdrich "Indian Boarding School: The Runaways"
> "Come to our reservation on the landfill to focus on waste and transcend...terminal creeds"
> Gerald Vizenor "Landfill Meditation"

D'Arcy McNickle's *The Surrounded* (1936) begins: "Archilde Leon had been away from his father's ranch for nearly a year." At the beginning of James Welch's *Winter in the Blood* (1974) the main character observes, "Coming home was not easy anymore." N. Scott Momaday's *House Made of Dawn* (1968) opens with the troubled homecoming of Abel, returning to his Pueblo village after fighting in World War II. Leslie Marmon Silko's *Ceremony*, (1977) also set in the aftermath of the Second World War, focuses on the lives of several Indian veterans returning home to their Laguna Reservation. In Louise Erdrich's *Love Medicine* (1984, 1993) the word "home" is found in the first sentence of the novel and it is the last word in the book. The opening story concerns June Kashpaw miles from home, but determined after an absence of many years to walk back to her Chippewa village, freezing to death on the snow-swept

Plains of North Dakota. Recently the Native Canadian writer Lee Maracle (Métis/Salish) has said "I don't write back, I write home."[2]

The theme of homecoming has clearly dominated contemporary Native North American writing. Homelessness, or the difficulty or even impossibility of coming home, are equally important themes, for exile, assimilation, marginality and dispossession of land and rights are today, and were in the past, very much part of the Native experience. Both *House Made of Dawn* and *Ceremony* start with the troubled return of a native son to the reservation after the Second World War, their traumatic memories of the overseas war adding to their sense of alienation. In *Ceremony* the returning Tayo is haunted by the memory of being ordered to fire on some Japanese prisoners, one of the Japanese faces turning into that of his beloved Uncle Josiah. In *Love Medicine* Henry Lamartine Junior, returning to his North Dakota Chippewa reservation from a prison of war camp in Vietnam, remembers a dying Vietcong girl pointing to his Asian-looking eyes and saying "You, me, same. Same" (176). The genetic link between North American Aboriginals and Asian peoples throws into sharp contrast the questions Tayo and Henry wrestle with: "Where is my home?;" "Is America my Home?;" and "Who did I fight for and for what reason?" The insistence on the themes of home and homelessness in contemporary Native North American writing is clear. What this essay will seek to define is why this theme is so insistent in Native American writing and the different forms and manifestations it can take.

Exile and homecoming are not of course unique to aboriginal experience. In his still useful essay "Reflections on Exile," Edward Said refers to Georg Lukács's *Theory of the Novel,* which persuasively argues that the novel is *the* form of "transcendental homelessness." The European novel, says Lukács, is essentially about an itinerant and disinherited middle-class hero seeking to reconstruct a new world that somewhat resembles an old one left behind for ever. But though this theory may well be true for the bourgeois European experience, it is plainly inadequate to encompass the aboriginal experience in North America, which involves different factors: primarily the dispossession of Native land and Native rights, and the difficulty or inability to cope with conflicting cultural patterns, leading all too frequently to alcoholism, violence and death. Salman Rushdie, like Lukács, also traces the connection between writing and homelessness. In his seminal essay "Imaginary Homelands" Rushdie makes it clear that the catalyst for his imagination is a return to a home of the mind, his childhood memories of Bombay, which are all the more intense because they are imaginary, products of a deceptive memory, rather than factual. Rushdie's version of the "Proustian ambition to unlock the gates of lost time" (Rushdie 10) is no doubt a universal urge, but again it does not truly encompass what we find with Native North American writers, primarily because Rushdie is very much concerned with an individual consciousness ("my" India, as he puts it), whereas time and again in Native North American writing there is an emphasis on the collective consciousness, the tribal as much as the individual experience.

In order to approach the Native North American sense of home it is necessary to listen to what Native people say about themselves. In "Coming Home Through Stories" Neal McLeod (Cree) opens his essay with these words:

> "To be home" means to dwell within the landscape of familiar, collective memories, as opposed to being in exile. "Being home" means to be a nation, to have access to land, to be able to raise your own children and to have political control. It involves a collective sense of dignity. In a post-colonial situation, by subverting the stories of the colonizer, one is able to reassert one's narratives. A collective memory emerges from a specific location, spatially and temporally, and includes such things as a relationship to land, songs, ceremonies, language and stories. (51)

What these definitions of home stress is the link between the individual and the collective experience. Note it is "collective memories" rather than individual memory that is stressed. McLeod also emphasises land, both as a specific location and as a resource from which communal values—"songs, ceremonies, language and stories"—spring. McLeod continues, "In contrast to 'being home,' diaspora is the process of being alienated from the collective memory of one's people," (52) and distinguishes between two kinds of diaspora: *spatial diaspora* (the removal of an Indigenous group from their land) and *ideological diaspora* (alienation from one's own stories). As McLeod rightly points out, spatial and ideological diaspora are interrelated and both are the product of the colonial presence. Certainly, the physical removal from the land (spatial diaspora) has been the historical experience of all Native North Americans, but today most Native writers would appear to be primarily concerned with ideological diaspora, often implicitly the preservation of cultural traditions, rather than with spatial diaspora in the sense of longing to return to a particular tribal homeland.

A number of reasons, then, can be given for the centrality of the theme of "home" in Native North American writing. Firstly, the historical removal of Aboriginal peoples from their land has created the need to "come home" through words, to repossess what has been lost through writing. This does not only mean writing about lost tribal land, but about the cultural memories and stories associated with that land. Secondly, coming home through stories helps counteract a sense of fragmentation and isolation. As Leslie Marmon Silko has written in "Language and Literature from a Pueblo Indian Perspective:" "The stories are always bringing us together, keeping this whole together, keeping this family together, keeping this clan together." Traditionally, these stories would be told orally, but increasingly today the medium of transmission is the written word. Thirdly, homecoming fictions by Native American writers have featured world events like the Second World War and the Vietnam War in which the Indian soldier hero who fought for his country returns to his native soil. These fictions foreground the marginalization of the protagonist and raise questions which ironise the notion of contemporary America as a "homeland" for Native Americans. In these works the Native people's historical experience of dispossession and removal from their own land is reprised in a twentieth century context.

I have suggested reasons why the theme of homecoming is so important, but that still leaves unanswered the question: what forms and manifestations does the theme take? In his useful essay "Opening the Text: *Love Medicine* and the Return of the Native American Woman," Robert Silberman discusses the notion of home in Native American literature. He sees the established canon of Native American literature, including D'Arcy McNickle's *The Surrounded,* N. Scott Momaday's *House Made of Dawn,* Leslie Marmon Silko's *Ceremony,* and James Welch's *Winter in the Blood* and *The Death of Jim Loney,* as in essence stories of a young man's troubled homecoming (101). He suggests that these writers can be seen as moving in the crosscurrents between oral tradition and the Western literary tradition, and that they use the theme of a young man's rite of passage (or failed rite of passage) as a symbolic representation of the tensions shared by the larger community (102). Silberman also makes the valid point that Louise Erdrich's *Love Medicine* is both part of this tradition and yet marks a break with it (103). In so far as *Love Medicine* is concerned with the consequences of an individual's return or attempted return to the reservation—as witnessed in the opening chapter of the novel where June Kashpaw returns home—and inasmuch as the novel deals with the significance of home and family, then Erdrich's work follows the tradition. But *Love Medicine* departs from the earlier novels represented by Momaday and others in that the central figure is a woman, not a man. Further, the narrative does not develop directly out of the problems caused by a return, (June Kashpaw freezes to death in the opening scene before she arrives home), rather it arises out of questions raised by the failed return; for example, "Who Killed June Kashpaw?" and "What Killed Her?" (103-4). To this should be added the point that whereas McNickle, Momaday, Silko and Welch open their works with protagonists who physically arrive "home," in Erdrich's work the opening fiction is about a spiritual rather than a physical homecoming. Though June's body freezes to death miles from home, her spirit returns:

> Even when her heart clenched and her skin turned crackling cold it didn't matter, because the pure and naked part of her went on.

> The snow fell deeper that Easter than it had in forty years, but June walked over it like water and came home (7).

Silberman's essay shows clearly that whether traditional literary patterns are adhered to or broken, nevertheless home and return are key themes in Native American literature. At the simplest level we have what might be called "bringing-them-home" fiction, like Richard Wagamese's *Keeper'n Me,* which shows a rootless Native man rediscovering his tribal identity by learning from Keeper, the Elder of the reserve, the old ways. Works by McNickle, Momaday, Welch and others of the "troubled homecoming" tradition are more complex and less programmatic. For them Native/non-Native life is not an either/or issue but a matter of cross-cultural tensions, conflicts *and* adjustments. Louise Erdrich takes the ambiguities and tensions of homecoming even further, giving the lie to Frost's dictum that home is the place where they have to take you in, or that home is necessarily the place where you want to be taken in. In *Love Medicine* the traditional dilemma of the individual is presented—home may be freedom, but it may also be a trap. The word "home" is continuously foregrounded, but notions like "home free," "something to come home to" and "no place like home" are continuously ironized. As Silberman says about *Love Medicine* "There's no place like home—but which one?" (108)

There is, of course, a wide range of responses by contemporary Native writers to the question of "home." To illustrate this I will look briefly at four recent works: Tomson Highway's *Kiss of the Fur Queen* (1998), Thomas King's *Green Grass, Running Water* (1993) and *Truth and Bright Water* (1999) and Gerald Vizenor's *Darkness in Saint Louis Bearheart* (1978, reprinted as *Bearheart: The Heirship Chronicles* in 1990).

Highway's *Kiss* problematises the notion of "home." As with Erdrich's poem "Indian Boarding School," home in *Kiss* is partly a childhood place of happiness the protagonist Jeremiah returns to in his dreams at residential school, dreams brutally shattered by the sexually abusive Principal of the school. But "home" is also the place he finds it increasingly difficult to return to as he grows older, cut off as he is from his parents by the barriers of his education and worldly experience—including two secrets from the outside world he can never confess—the sexual abuse by Father Lafleur at the Catholic school and his brother Gabriel's homosexuality. In the case of the former, the brothers know that their parents' Catholicism is so unshakable that "Even if we told them, they would side with Father Lafleur" (92). "Home" here mirrors the power structures of a world in which the victim is disbelieved and evil is allowed to flourish. With the latter, when Gabriel's promiscuous homosexuality (a product of his sexual initiation by Lafleur) leads to his contracting AIDS, his condition literally becomes "unspeakable:" "How do you say AIDS in Cree, huh? Tell me, what's the word for HIV" (296) Gabriel says to his brother. AIDS becomes a "home truth" that can never be spoken.

Highway's novel could thus be seen as yet another example of the "troubled homecoming" tradition of Native literature, except that the notion of "home" is not limited to geographical place (a farm, a reservation, and so on) but has a mythical or, to use McLeod's terminology, an "ideological" dimension. Except in postmodern texts which defy closure, notions of home are most likely to be clarified at the end of works of fiction, when the work itself "comes home" to rest. In the final chapter of *Kiss*, Jeremiah "comes home" to his cultural roots at the death bed of his brother, Gabriel, when he initiates the sweetgrass purification ceremonies of the Cree and slams the door in the Catholic priest's face. But the ultimate finale comes when the Fur Queen, a female trickster figure based primarily on the androgynous Cree trickster Weesageechak, arrives to take Gabriel to his spiritual home: "Rising from his body, Gabriel Okimasis and the Fur Queen floated off into the swirling mist, as the little white fox on the collar of the cape turned to Jeremiah. And winked" (306).

Gabriel's death is symptomatic on the individual level of the effect of the Christian Church on the lives of Aboriginals worldwide. But note here that the Fur Queen, or rather her synecdochic symbol, the white fox fur, winks at Jeremiah, as if passing on a message of optimism in the face of catastrophe. "Home" here is associated with cultural survival kept alive by transmission of what Highway calls "The dream world of North American Indian mythology," foremost among these "fantastic creatures" being the Trickster (see "A Note on the Trickster," Highway's preface to all his published work).

King's *Green Grass, Running Water* is also about homecoming. On one level it is a realistic fiction about returning to Native roots, shown by the convergence of all the main characters on the town of Blossom, Alberta for the annual Sun Dance. It is also about standing firm on one's Native soil in the face of corporate and government pressure to appropriate Indian land, as shown by the success of Eli Stands Alone in standing up against the Grand Baleen Dam project. But here again there is clearly also a "mythical level" in the novel. Throughout the work Coyote attempts to tell the tale of the origin of the world, a tale that not only interrupts the smooth flow of the narrative, but is itself continuously interrupted. The novel begins and ends with Genesis, or rather the Gospel. According to Coyote: "In the beginning, there was nothing just the water" (1, 469). King's work is an example of what Vizenor has called "Trickster discourse," where master narratives, plots, identities, stereotypes, the status quo and dominant norms are all subverted through textual play that is both postmodern and also part of the oral tradition of Native Trickster tales. It is the same point that Neal McLeod is making in "Coming Home Through Stories:" "In a post-colonial situation, by subverting the stories of the colonizer, one is able to reassert one's (own) narratives" (51).

Central to King's most recent novel, *Truth and Bright Water*, is the homecoming of the local hero, Munroe Swimmer. Swimmer is a trickster artist who, returning to the town of Bright Water sets about returning the land to its pre-contact days. Purchasing the "Sacred Word Gospel Church," he repaints it so that it disappears and becomes seamlessly merged with the prairie landscape. In effect, the missionary presence, the sacred word, is erased, to be replaced by the language of Native forms. Swimmer also installs iron buffaloes in the landscape and they come alive and repopulate the prairies once again. King's novel clearly has parallels with the "troubled homecoming" tradition in Native American writing—Lum, one of the young Indian protagonists in *Truth and Bright Water*, searches for his lost mother (a link with the character of Tayo in Silko's *Ceremony*) but at the end of the novel commits suicide by diving in the water (a parallel here with the death of Henry Lamartine Junior in Erdrich's *Love Medicine*). The importance of healing—not only coming home to the tribe, but dealing with the conflicting demands of different cultures—also connects King with Momaday, Silko and Erdrich. Abel's healing in *House Made of Dawn* begins with the Navajo night chant which centres him in "the house made of dawn"—the Navajo universe in which mind, body and voice are restored. Tayo in *Ceremony* is eventually restored to wholeness through healing chants and ceremonies. In *Truth and Bright Water* the main protagonist Tecumseh will in the future become the ceremonial storyteller of Munroe Swimmer's trickster antics, which have brought about empowerment through literally transforming and recreating the landscape. As Munroe says to Tecumseh: "Minstrels sing about heroes and great deeds. ...You have to make up songs and stories about me so that no one forgets who I am" (193).

To move from Momaday and Silko to the work of Gerald Vizenor is to go from the realm of realistic fiction into a postmodern world in which long-cherished beliefs about Native Americans begin to dissolve. In the public imagination the so-called "Indian problem" is very much about the legal status of homelands, and revolves around issues such a treaty rights, trust status and tribal sovereignty. For Vizenor, however, the destiny of the American Indian rests not with notions of "home" and land rights, but with language. The conflict is between popular, scientific, literary and political rhetoric versus tribal oral tradition. Notions of "Indianness," as Berkhofer (1979) and Francis (1992) have shown, is a construct invented by non-Native peoples. "Indianness" is the imposition of a false notion of nationhood; it is cultural destruction though stereotype. Vizenor's weapons in the war of cultural survival are words, and he has invented a number of neologisms to describe this battle: *word warriors, postindian warriors of survivance, wordarrows,* and so on. One of his most productive terms is "terminal creeds," that is, closed and static ideas that like diseases can be fatal. One of the well-known "terminal creeds" is the notion that the Indian is somehow "attached to the land;" it is, to Vizenor, an idea that too narrowly interpreted could be fatal to the cultural survival of Native Americans. In Vizenor's first novel *Darkness in Saint Louis Bearheart* one of the female characters named Belladonna Darwin-Winter Catcher is asked to define "tribal values." She replies with a series of clichés "We are tribal and that means that we are children of dreams and visions. ...Our bodies are connected to mother earth and our minds are part of the clouds. ...Our voices are the living breath of the wilderness" (190), and so on. Belladonna is eventually poisoned and dies for the sake of her static beliefs. As the trickster-like Proude Cedarfair comments, "We become our memories and what we believe. ...We become the terminal creeds we speak" (143). The fictional protagonist of Vizenor's short story "Landfill Meditation," Martin Bear Charme, can be regarded as the contrary of Belladonna. Bear Charme is a woodland Indian who finds himself transported to an urban environment. Refusing to fulfil the usual Indian stereotypes (unemployment, alcoholism, violent behaviour, and so on) he gets a job and eventually makes his fortune "hauling trash and filling wetlands with urban swill and solid waste" (100). A modern-day trickster (tricksters are often associated with excrement), Bear Charme adapts to the urban conditions without a romanticized longing for the land or the past, unencumbered by terminal creeds. "Come to our reservation on the landfill to focus on waste and transcend...terminal creeds" (105), he says.

The prevailing theme of home and homecoming in Native North American fiction takes many forms including realistic, ironic, and deconstructive modes. "Coming home," too, can mean many things: a return to an actual place, a homeland, a tribe, the reservation, or it can involve a return to a place of memory, ceremony, song and myth. Gerald Vizenor would appear to break the mould, but in fact his work too concerns reclamation and coming home, namely the construction of a self free of cultural impositions and stereotypes. All the works discussed concern dispossession, whether it be dispossession of land, stories, culture or language; they also concern the repossession of self and identity—a coming home through words.

NOTES

1. This essay is an expanded and elaborated version of one section of an article entitled, "Native North American Writing and Postcolonialism" (*Hungarian Journal of English and American Studies*, forthcoming 2002).
2. Lee Maracle, speaking at a public reading of her work at the 23rd Annual Conference of the Association for the Study of the New Literatures in English, Aachen, June 2000.

WORKS CITED

Berkhofer, Robert F. Jr. *The White Man's Indian: Images of the American Indian from Columbus to the Present.* New York: Vintage, 1979.

Erdrich, Louise. *Love Medicine.* New York: Perennial, 2001.

Francis, Daniel. *The Imaginary Indian: The Image of the Indian in Canadian Culture.* Vancouver: Arsenal Pulp, 1992.

Highway, Tomson. *Kiss of the Fur Queen.* Toronto: Doubleday, 1998.

King, Thomas. *Green Grass, Running Water.* New York: Bantam, 1994.

——. *Truth and Bright Water.* New York: Atlantic Monthly Press, 1999.

McLeod, Neal. "Coming Home Through Stories." *International Journal of Canadian Studies* 18 (1998): 51-66.

McNickle, D'Arcy. *The Surrounded.* Albuquerque: U New Mexico P, 1964.

Momaday, N. Scott. *House Made of Dawn.* New York: Perennial, 1977.

Rushdie, Salman. "Imaginary Homelands." *Imaginary Homelands: Essays and Criticism 1981-1991.* London: Penguin Books, 1991. 9-21.

Said, Edward. "Reflections on Exile." *Out There: Marginalization and Contemporary Cultures.* Ed. R. Ferguson et al. Cambridge, Mass.: MIT Press, 1990. 357-66.

Silberman, Robert. "Opening the Text: *Love Medicine* and the Return of the Native American Woman." *Narrative Chance: Postmodern Discourse on Native American Indian Literatures.* Ed. Gerald Vizenor. Norman: U of Oklahoma P, 1993.

Silko, Leslie Marmon. *Ceremony.* New York: Viking Press, 1977.

——. "Language and Literature from a Pueblo Indian Perspective." *Yellow Woman and a Beauty of the Spirit: Essays on Native American Life Today.* New York: Simon and Schuster, 1996.

Vizenor, Gerald. *Darkness in Saint Louis Bearheart.* St. Paul, Minn.: Truck Press, 1978. Rpt. as *Bearheart: The Heirship Chronicles.* Minneapolis: U of Minnesota P, 1990.

——. "Landfill Meditation." *Landfill Meditation: Crossblood Stories.* Hanover, N.H.: Wesleyan UP/UP of New England, 1991. 98-115.

Wagamese, Richard. *Keeper'n Me.* Toronto: Doubleday, 1994.

Welch, James. *Winter in the Blood.* New York: Penguin, 1986.

——. *The Death of Jim Loney.* New York: Harper and Row, 1979.

4

Justifying Sethe's Act in Toni Morrison's *Beloved*

RASHMI GAUR

Beloved is a saga of grit and courage, a chronicle of fundamental contradictions which always define a civilization; the subtext of survival instinct, subconscious urge towards domesticity and belonging, and the basic human need to grab emotional and physical sustenance wherever and howsoever possible is also evident in the structure of the novel—but what becomes most significantly transparent is the moving combination of the strength and constraints of a woman who is basically a mother, and happens to be a black slave in a society which is bifurcated by dominant racial hatred into two sections—the ruler and the ruled, the master and the slave, at a turbulent time of the American history. This Pulitzer prize winning novel cannot be interpreted in a simplistic manner. Among the different layers of probable meanings involving a multi-leveled communication which has always existed between the reader and the text, the most significantly loaded meaning/impression the reader retains is of a mother struggling to save her children from a predictable brutal future—a black woman who has faced the cruelty on her race at first hand, who has been cow-hided and emotionally deshaped before spending only 28 days of tentative freedom in the company of her children, mother-in-law and neighbours, trying desperately to protect her children from the repetitive fate of her race, a person hounded by generations of future—obliterating terror acting decisively to put her babies "where they'd be safe" (Morrison 201). This impression, retained by a reader, is further intensified by the fact that Morrison herself has refused to take sides. Using the flashback technique, she has contrived to put across certain sympathy for Sethe, but has restrained herself from direct and conclusive denouement in terms of justifying Sethe's choice of slashing her infant daughter's throat rather than see it in chains. This authorial act has added a sense of ethical responsibility to the reader's hermeneutic response to the text—each reader has to internalize the facts of the narrative and take a decision in terms of defending or rejecting Sethe's choice. Again, the decision perhaps can never be an easy one—the reader will have to critically review many personal beliefs and values before arriving at a decision, even then neither the defence nor the rejection will ever be completely categorical. The decision howsoever ambiguous it is, will also be a commentary on the reader's commitments.

Motherhood has always universally been riddled with traditional interpretations and pre-conditioned view-points. Even a thinker like Simone de Beauvoir has termed it as a natural calling for a woman as it fulfils her physiological destiny (*SS* 501). The male psyche subconsciously and unobtrusively adds the psychological destiny too, to this interpretation. This interpretation is correct in a limited manner as within normal surroundings a woman values the child more than her own self. Her own value as an individual is relegated to the background, and the child and its needs take precedence, particularly when the child as an infant, is dependent on its mother for its security and life. The violation and destruction of this bond, which is a cultural pre-condition of the mother-child relationship in all societies will tear the familial fabric asunder. But while portraying an intense and sensitive love of a mother towards her children, *Beloved* definitely does not present any normal backdrop.

In order to understand the fullest implications of *Beloved*, the narrative of which is set in 1873, the reader will have to understand the bizarre social set-up of contemporary America. The atrocities which were committed on slaves then are common history now. But while history reveals situational facts, it also suppresses sensitivity towards individuals living through those situations. Literature alone can unravel the intricacies of experiential patterns which an individual had to suffer while history was being made. Sethe's predicament is able to focus simultaneously on various traumas a slave woman was to undergo before the abolition of slavery in America. The narrative of *Beloved* is made more authentic and poignant by the fact that its main incident is based on a real historically recorded event. Quoting from an interview with Morrison, Mervyn Rothstein in her newspaper article "Toni Morrison, in her new novel, defends women," mentions the incident which moved her to write the novel; in Morrison's own words, "I was amazed by this story I came across about a woman called Margaret Garner who had escaped from Kentucky, I think, into Cincinnati with four children. And she was a kind of cause celebre among abolitionists in 1855 or '56 because she tried to kill the children when she was caught. She killed one of them, just as in the novel. I found an article in a magazine of the period, and there was this young woman in her 20's, being interviewed and she was very calm, she was very serene. They kept remarking on the fact that she was not frothing at the mouth, she was not a mad woman, and she kept saying, 'No, the're not going to live like that. They will not live the way I have lived;" the picture of life which comes through this statement is ugly, empty and dreadful. The echo of Hamlet's words to Horatio in the grave digging scene can be felt in the statement of the mother. Surrounded by death and destruction in their ugliest manifestation a mother consciously severs that thread of life which she herself had brought into this world. The deeper, unfathomable feelings which had formed the basis of this decision leave the reader flabbergasted initially, as in order to come to terms to this act, he will have to assuage the depth of a mother's love trying desperately to create defensive barriers amongst attitudes of pathetic diablerie, to safeguard her children who are more valuable than her own person. Rothstein further quotes Morrison: "I did a lot of research about everything else in the book—Cincinnati, and abolitionists, and the underground railroad—but I refused to find out anything else about Margaret Garner. I really wanted to invent her life. I had a few important things—the sex of the children, how many there were, and the fact that she succeeded in cutting the throat of one and that she was about to bash another one's head up against the wall when someone stopped her. The rest was novel writing. I don't know if that story came because I was considering certain aspects of self-sabotage, the ways in which the best things we do so often carry seeds of one's own destruction" (MR 1). Through *Beloved* Morrison has been able to successfully catch the dual emotions of clearly perceptible anger and muted compassion, leaving the difficult task of making an ethical decision on her readers.

Sethe has once remarked in the novel, "Unless carefree, motherlove was a killer" (162). Her own experiences of slavery act constantly as reference points in the narrative. As a child and also as a grown up woman Sethe often wonders about her own mother. Her mother was brought into a plantation from Africa and used as a milking cow by the slavers. She had also thrown all her children into sea except Sethe. But her rejection of her newly born children had an altogether different reason. She disowned her children from the crew and the white men, protecting only Sethe and giving her the name of the black man she had that child from. Her rejection was caused by hatred and pride—hatred towards a race of exploiters and pride to perpetuate her own racial identity, while Sethe's act has resulted from the compulsive love of a mother to safeguard her children's future.

Sethe's trauma unfolds gradually in Sweet Home, a farm in Kentucky, kept by Garner as a model of good ownership. She is a slave here like the Pauls, Halle and Sixo; a slave as Baby Suggs had been till her freedom was purchased by her son at the cost of his own life. Morrison has used stream of consciousness technique suggestively to reveal the details of this plantation in snippets. Here Sethe loves and marries Halle and tries to create a tentative home so long as Garner is alive. Her efforts, "though superficially consoling, fail, and in their failure point to the real barriers facing Sethe in self-actualization and home-making" (NJ 3). The atrocities and mental trauma Sethe had to face in Sweet Home chronicle the total subjugation of a race which was made a victim of coercion, sexism and racism, practised successfully to obliterate their individuality. Garner's policy of containment allowed Sethe and other slaves to exercise a limited self-hood. He is presented as an enlightened slaver who allowed his slaves certain choices in an environment when choices were non-existent. The choices of buying liberty to a mother, handling guns, even learning to read and moving freely inside the property provide the semblance of a limited freedom. The Sweet Home under Garner and the Sweet Home under the rule of Schoolteacher are two different entities. The basic tenets of slave culture are latent in Garner's approach but it shall be an injustice to say that despite different styles, the two men shared the same grammar of chattel slavery (NJ 2). He possesses the individuals and extracts their labour, but he does not physically maltreats them. His plantation did not promise any freedom to his slaves, but it definitely held out a promise of a well fed and secure existence. Baby Suggs admits before the Bodwins that she had not lived in a place better than the Ganer's plantation (Morrison 179). Sethe is able to escape the tragedy of being separated from her children so long as Garner is there, whereas Baby Suggs had to undergo this traumatic experience seven times, "The last of her children, whom she barely glanced at when he was born because it wasn't worth the trouble to try to learn features you would never see change into adulthood anyway. Seven times she had done that: held a little foot; examined the fat fingertips with her own—fingers she never saw become the male or female hands a mother would recognize anywhere. She didn't know to this day what their permanent teeth looked like; or how they held their heads when they walked. Did Patty lose her lisp? What color did Famous' skin finally take? Was that a cleft in Johnny's chin or just a dimple that would disappear soon's his jawbone changed?" (Morrison 171). Sethe could enjoy Buglar's and Howard's childhood, their running up and rolling down the patches. She has had the "amazing luck of six whole years of marriage to that 'somebody' son who had fathered everyone of her children" (Morrison 29). The atmosphere changes under the Schoolteacher and his two nephews. Sethe and other slaves realize that definitions belong to the definers (Morrison 234), as they are gradually deprived of their guns, game and food and are reduced to a state when pilfering becomes not only their right but also their obligation (Morrison 234). Soon afterwards Sethe overhears the Schoolteacher asking his pupil to divide and line up her human and animal characteristics, in order to grasp the definition of property. Mrs. Garner's definition of the word characteristics— "a thing that's natural to a thing" (Morrison 239)—confirms her worst fears. "She is the udder they drink from and the sexual body they work their pleasures on—adjusting her characteristics to whatever shape their fantasies demand. That is, the white schoolboys'/nephews' fantasies of 'animal characteristics' are played out on Sethe's too human body. Under Schoolteacher's tutelage, the pupils learn to turn people into animals" (NJ 4). The horror of the situation gradually sinks into the slaves' psyche enabling and encouraging them to plan their escape to the magical North, "That way," says Halle, "Where he took my ma'am. Sixo say freedom is that way. A whole train is going and if we can get there, don't need to be no buy-out" (Morrison 242). Their experiences with the ugly face of slavery goad them into planning their escape. When it is time to translate the plan into action, six "buts" interrupt and the plan goes awry (Morrison 274-75). Sixo is burned up, Paul D is dressed in a collar, Halle disappears, a body with Paul A's shirt on but without his feet or head is hanged in the trees and Sethe is taken to the barn for sport. The pupils never believed that Sethe would be able to run away as she was crippled by her belly and by her back. But Sethe manages to send her children towards safety, to Baby Suggs and follows them herself. Defying the slave system Sethe acts like a mother, "Nobody going to keep me from my children" (Morrison 248). The determination to be with her children enables her to brave the rough passage, endure the birth pangs and have her first glimpses of freedom. She concurs with Paul D when he says that "to get to a place where you could love anything you chose—not to need permission for desire—well now that was freedom" (Morrison 199). As a slave she did not have either the right or the permission to enjoy any pleasure— even the mist, doves, sunlight, copper dirt, moon "belonged to the men who had the guns" (Morrison 199). Sethe had loved Halle as she was permitted to do so, she had loved her children in the plantation because they were not snatched away from her, because she was permitted to keep them. An awareness of limitations and defined boundaries had kept that love somehow confined, limited and incomplete. Only when she crosses over to safety and freedom, she realizes what it is to love freely. Even her relationship with her children changes: "Look like I loved em more after I got here. Or may be I couldn't love em proper in Kentucky because they wasn't mine to love" (Morrison 199). This sense of elation was not possible in the Sweet Home. The juxtaposition of these two states makes her aware of their inherent qualitative difference, confirming her faith that she will never allow any of her children to live under a sadistic slave owner: "I couldn't let all that go back to where it was, and I couldn't let her nor any of 'em live under Schoolteacher. That was out'" (Morrison 200). Trembling on the verge of half apprehended freedom, Sethe has generic and deep-rooted fears. Despite the imprint of the choke-cherry tree on her back, she was able to deliver Denver and create life anew by thwarting the designs of the slavers. Yet this grit and resilience are not able to mitigate her fears for her children. She wants them to be free, actually free. What we get is the picture of a mother, fiercely determined to protect her children from a future which will unfold only as a repetition of her past.

Ironically, a mother who loves her children so deeply, is pushed to a corner where she sees no other way but to kill them in order to save them from the banalities of life, from tree cages, collars, ankle ropes and wells. When she sees the Schoolteacher and the Sheriff coming towards the house, she immediately visualizes what the future life has in store for her children and she revolts. She does not want to surrender her children to the cruelty perpetuated on her: "when she saw them coming and recognized schoolteacher's hat, she heard wings. Little hummingbirds stuck their needle beaks right through her headcloth into her hair and beat their wings. And if she thought anything, it was No. No. Nono. Nonono. Simple. She just flew. Collected every bit of life she had made, all the parts of her that were precious and fine and beautiful, and carried, pushed, dragged them through the veil, out, away, over there where no one could hurt them. Over there. Outside this place, where they would be safe" (Morrison 200). This was the only way she could perceive of thwarting the Schoolteacher's brutality, his designs of taking back her children and raising them to do the work Sweet Home desperately needed. When she comes out of the jail she still has some satisfaction, "I stopped him, I took and put my babies where they'd be safe" (Morrison 201).

Sethe constantly recalls her past, as if by doing so she would be able to free herself from its horrors. The past constantly haunts her, the Sweet Home comes back whether she wanted it or not. *Beloved* is a novel "about the traumas and healing powers of memory, or 'rememory' as Sethe calls it, adding a connotation of cyclical recurrence. Sethe's ambivalent relationship to her cruel past creates a kind of wavelike narrative effect, as memories surface and are repressed" (KD 6). The past is reenacted for Sethe, when Bodwin, who has come to pick up Denver, is perceived as a reincarnation of the Schoolteacher and attacked with an icepick at the end of the novel.

This attack, as well as the attempt to kill the white man is a mother's reaction to protect her children. For a mother, her children are always more precious than her own self. Besides, a mother is always more protective towards her daughter as compared to that of a son, as a girl can be exploited in multiple ways. Sethe wants her daughters and sons to escape a future which refuses to look at them as human beings, assessing their value only as objects. The reaction of the Schoolteacher after Sethe has attempted killing her children bears testimony to it. He is dejected because the children, "pickaninnies," who were needed to work on the farm are not fit any more, "Two were lying open-eyed in saw-dust, a third pumped blood down the dress of the main one- the woman schoolteacher bragged about, the one he said made fine ink, damn good soup, pressed his collars the way he liked besides having at least ten breeding years left. But now she'd gone wild, due to the mishandling of the nephew who'd overbeat her and made her cut and run. Schoolteacher had chastised that nephew, telling him to think—just think-what would his own horse do if you beat it beyond the point of education...suppose you beat the hounds past that point that away. Never again could you trust them in the woods or anywhere else—see what happened when you overbeat the creatures..." (Morrison 184). The Schoolteacher does not differentiate between a slave and other animals. He has no compassion for the children, as they are understood as property only. His indifference to the outcome of his own cruelty startles us into a new awareness of the evils of a system, the aftereffects of which can be felt even in contemporary America. An awareness of these implications pushes Sethe instinctively to commit a subhuman act, but the act itself cannot be taken out of its context and condemned vociferously. What she has done is done for the best motives—having tasted freedom herself, albeit for 28 days only, her only desire is to put her children in a safe place, safe from the racist atrocities she had to face, "she (Beloved) had to be safe and I put her where she would be" (Morrison 246).

Mother love displaces the self, Morrison has said, "The precious interior, the loved self, whatever that is, whatever vocabulary you ascribe to it, is suppressed or displaced and put someplace else—in the children, in the lover, in the man. It's always something other that is more valuable, more beautiful, more wonderful than the self...it's just that they [children] become what she says in the book, that that's the best part of me. That's what maternity is" (MR 2). In a system which denies parenthood Sethe wants to be a mother, wants to protect her children. She is defying a system and hence easily misunderstood. Paul D's judgement that Sethe's love is "too thick" is a misunderstanding because though he is familiar with the evils of slavery, he "does not know what it is like to be both parent and slave, let alone both mother and slave" (JP 9). He is thinking as a slave, not as a slave-mother who could never have any true safety in her life.

Though Morrison has vividly presented the cruelties perpetuated on slaves, she has determinedly refused to take sides as far as justification of Sethe's act/choice is concerned. She neither endorses Sethe's view of her own action, nor Paul D's, nor the Schoolteacher's. The total absence of any authorial comment transfers the responsibility of decoding the textual message to the reader in a significant way. James Phelan comments, "At the level of author-audience communication, Morrison's unusual treatment of Sethe's choice also creates an unusual ethical relationship with her audience. The treatment is simultaneously a challenge and a compliment. She challenges us to have the negative capability to refrain from any irritable reaching after ethical closure about Sethe's rough choice, even as that challenge implies her faith that we will be equal to the task—by accepting that responsibility—and attending to the parameters within which Morrison asks us to exercise it—we have a more difficult and demanding but also richer reading experience. By guiding us less, Morrison gives us more" (JP 10).

Sethe merits our sympathy. She has been pushed to the limits of human tolerance and has reacted to it instinctively, trying all the while to protect her children. The system has put her in a situation where protecting her children means murdering them. Extraordinary situations call for extraordinary responses which cannot and should not be judged from the view-point of ordinary behaviour. Her rough choice is motivated by an inner compassion, which is manifested in the only channel of action available to her. It cannot be condemned; rather, her choice, the dilemma of her motherhood, and her tainted liberation later on, compel the reader to condemn the system of slavery, which can have such effect on human lives. *Beloved* is not only an indictment of the past, it is also a resurrection of history in a fictional mode which reminds us that the institution of slavery has continued to grip the psyche of the African Americans till today, who want to exorcise it while keeping their historical consciousness alive. Within this context of resolving a historical trauma, *Beloved* suggestively puts forth a mother's resolute, unqualified and unflinching love towards her children.

WORKS CITED

de Beauvoir, Simone. *The Second Sex* (Berkshire, UK: Vintage, 1997). Referred to in the text as *SS*.

Jesser, Nancy. "Violence, home and community in Toni Morrison's *Beloved*." *African American Review*. 10 Sept. 2001. <http://www.findarticles.com/cf_0/m2838/2_33/55577123/p1/article.jhtml?term=Toni+Morrison>. Referred to in the text as NJ.

Morrison, Toni. *Beloved.* New York: Signet Printing, 1991.

Phelan, James. "Sethe's choice: *Beloved* and the ethics of reading." *Style.* 10 Sept. 2001. <http://www.findarticles.com/cf_0/m2342/2_32/54637198/p1/article.jhtml?term=Toni+Morrison>. Referred to in the text as JP.

Rothstein, Cindy Mervyn. "Toni Morrison, In Her New Novel, Defends Women (1987)." *NY Times.* 10 Sept. 2001. <http://www.nytimes.com/books/98/01/11/home/14013.html>. Referred to in the text as MR.

5

Recent American Poetry Anthologies: Contrastive Statements on Poetics and Constant Elements in Poetic Construction

MANUEL BRITO

The proliferation of American poetry anthologies in the last two decades has made it clear that wider cultural issues lie behind their appearance. The almost simultaneous publication of some anthologies within a short period, reflecting various modes of writing and different ideological leanings shows the variety of our contemporary society as well as the rapid changes currently taking place in the United States. A rich variety of cultural approaches, a great abundance of innovative formulations and thoughts can be found, sparkling in the pages of these anthologies. There are selections from various historical periods, poets from different backgrounds and texts which illustrate the fullness of the fin-de-siècle experience. A common criticism of most anthologies is centered upon which writers are left out or which work is most representative of those included. To this end, the combination of personal taste and the intention of covering everything collapse, revealing the process of constructing the anthology together with literary preferences and social attitudes. Usually the policy is to mark a defined territory through the extracts taken from those considered the best or most representative authors, arranged according to subject, in chronological order or listed alphabetically, sometimes with biographical notes providing basic information on the poets. Of course the creative work takes on a primary significance but some of these recent anthologies have included a valuable section on poetics, giving the reader an exact dimension of that construction and helping us fix our attention on those featured in the anthology. This strategy was used by Donald M. Allen in his seminal anthology, *The New American Poetry: 1945-1960* (1960), where the section "Statements on Poetry" plays a significant role. Curiously enough, when anthologists of the 1980s and 90s re-took that section on poetics for the construction of their collection, they followed the same aesthetic approach as Allen's, which opted for an avant-garde poetry, in opposition to academic verse. Besides this, these short essays on the truth and nature of poetry establish a clear link between the reader and the poet in considering the -isms as well as the individual concerns governing the poetic discipline.

It is true that some so-called innovative or experimental anthologies have been directed to a smaller and marginal audience: primarily poets, critics and a few readers belonging to specific literary milieu. This is due to the less effective marketing strategy of some of the small presses which published these anthologies or to the difficulties created by some new poetical proposals demanding a basic training. The reasons given by Hank Lazer to the question of why we need to produce anthologies sheds light on this. Firstly: economy, allowing readers to easily obtain such variety, which otherwise would require buying several books and spending more. Secondly, anthologies are great tools for teaching, as they illustrate the conflicts within each country's cultural scene, although this is not always the case nowadays since some anthologies prefer to be limited to particular literary tendencies or to a cluster of poets sharing common aims. However, generally speaking, "anthologies reinforce the fragmentation of the world, and wittingly or unwittingly, reinscribe the non-conversation at large" (Lazer 142). Needless to say, they have become even more useful when they include statements or discursive notes on poetics that definitely help us to see that the poem itself comes first. This may be because these are written by the poets who usually tend not to write about a program of reading as most critics do, but to develop the emerging theme or spirit of the text. In such writing, although we sometimes find extremely abstract speculations, we are more often invited to see the other side of writing practice.

Criticism from this perspective comes not only from critics, but from poets who propose their own aesthetic model and urge critics to question about their role as custodians or interpreters of our cultural heritage.[1] In the last two decades, the publication of books of criticism with such essays on poetics by the poets themselves has in fact been prolific. Some collections of essays mainly by innovative poetry practitioners should be mentioned: Michael Palmer's edition of *Code of Signals: Recent Writings in Poetics* (1983), *The L=a=n=g=u=a=g=e Book* (1984) edited by Bruce Andrews and Charles Bernstein, Bob Perelman's *Writings/Talks* (1985), Robert Frank's and Henry Sayre's *The Line in Postmodern Poetry* (1988), James McCorkle's *Conversant Essays: Contemporary Poets on Poetry* (1990), Charles Bernstein's *The Politics of Poetic Form* (1990), and *A Poetics of Criticism* (1994) edited by Juliana Spahr, Mark Wallace, Kristin Prevallet and Pam Rehm, or more recently Christopher Beach's collection entitled *Artifice & Indeterminacy: An Anthology of New Poetics* (1998). This trend also extends to formalist tendencies as evidenced by the publications of Frederick Feirstein's *Expansive Poetry: Essays on the New Narrative and New Formalism* (1989) and Robert McDowell's edition of *After Modernism* (1991). All aim at these essays answering the questions which encourage poets to look for the creative *poiesis*. The scope is wide, ranging from radical proposals to the most conventional issues in poetry but all these books illustrate the wider than ever variety of active formulas in use in the American poetic scene.

Experimental poets who most obviously descend from the line of Pound-Zukofsky-Olson are the most emphatic in strengthening a decentered poetics. Their essays on the subject have not only been included in the above publications but also in numerous magazines and academic journals, defining their particular programs and re-transmitting them for the vitality of this literary discipline. They do an excellent job of scrubbing and polishing exhausted poetical areas, trying to find new modes of perception and writing procedures. In the last two decades, three anthologies have offered a combination of creative or primary work and poetics essays: Ron Silliman's *In the American Tree* (1986), *Primary Trouble: An Anthology of Contemporary American Poetry* (1996) edited by Leonard Schwartz, Joseph Donahue and Edward Foster, and Mary M. Sloan's *Moving Borders: Three Decades of Innovative Writing by Women* (1998). Of the 119 poets included in these anthologies, the most recurrent poets are, Susan Howe and Bernadette Mayer, who appear in all of these three developing ideas aligned with disjunctive techniques.

Generally speaking, these anthologies share many aspects: individuation of intentions (though some of them belonged to specific poetic trends), challenges about style and ideology, assignation of a political role to the act of writing and reading, remarks about the paragraph and the line, and new statements on the relationship between language and its representation. *The New American Poetry* appears as the closest antecedent of these anthologies; not only as it celebrates the intersection between poetry and poetics, but also because Donald M. Allen included poets who defy the limits of poetry. Allen selected and evaluated the inclusion of poets challenging the existing poetical canon, who have tried to heighten the contrast between cooked and raw poetry. Perhaps with the intention of preserving a poetry that had been mainly published by small presses and little magazines. Preservation cannot be considered in the same terms as when Alan C. Golding refers back to the 18th and 19th-century American poetry anthologies, "selecting from abundance, protecting from oblivion,"[2] since Allen had the clear intention of selecting those few poets who reacted against standard values, who were using open forms as a way of liberation, and adding a new range of strategies in response to the demands of the new situation provided by post-war social and artistic consciousness. In so selecting, Allen also preserved what was scattered and diluted in pamphlets, little magazines and small presses, giving us a documentary view of the period. It is true that this anthology was compiled to suit his personal taste, but the main intention was to provide a voice to those experiments woven from Charles Olson up to David Meltzer. The first link between the selected poets was a rejection of academic verse to follow the innovations of Ezra Pound and William C. Williams, allied with arts other than poetry. Therefore, the main aim was "to give the reader some sense of the history of the period and primary alignment of the writers" (Allen xii). In order to better understand that literary history, he included some statements on poetics which "lead directly back to the poems, to the actual work of the period, waiting to be read and studied for what it alone can reveal" (Allen xiv).

Possibly Allen's main purpose was not to earn money, but to introduce a new poetic work to be used either purely for reading pleasure or for teaching purposes. He nevertheless joins the other conventional anthologists in presenting a larger audience with a collection of poets who struggle against the mainstream and consequently deserve more attention. The "difference" consists of the insertion of new "poetic" theories along with new practices that inform us refreshingly of the wider possibilities of poetic creation.[3] Another striking development is the new status acquired by this proposed diverse poetic approach in the following decades. This anthology thus catalyzed a wider acceptance of anthologies, simultaneously covering various poetic scopes and trends or focusing on specific, previously unusual issues and themes. Indeed, new anthologies range from the provocative—ascribed to specific reading venues, like Anne Waldman's *Out of This World: An Anthology of the St. Mark's Poetry Project, 1966-1991* (1991), through regional poets like *Practicing Angels: A Contemporary Anthology of San Francisco Bay Area Poetry* (1986), edited by Michael Mayo, or the accepted combination of multiculturalism and feminism in Barbara Smith's *Home Girls: A Black Feminist Anthology* (1983). In any case, Allen opened up the possibilities and favored a view of poetry as essentially experimental, and demolished versifiers aligned with strict formal approaches attached to academic standards, or with winning the Book of the Month Club prizes.

A new generation of poets who challenge poetic norms,

constantly experimenting with new forms became clearly established because of that anthology. The rapid succession of poetic movements holding on to this intention of continuing to be radical in their writings, and their progressively more frequent appearance in print are clear signs of the key role of the anthology in the American poetic scene. It is also symptomatic of the heterogeneity of open poetry and its adoption in the last few decades, as exemplified by poetic movements like Deep Image, Ethnopoetics, concrete and visual poetry, performance poetry, language poetry and, to some extent, the elliptical poets. Of course, Allen's anthology has not been the only stimulus to new interest in openness and wider acceptance of innovative modes in the literary America of recent decades. The spread of more easily accessible printing techniques, the academic absorption of many poets by the university system as well as the funding provided by the National Endowment for the Arts have also definitely helped towards this boom in experimentalism. Jonathan Holden refers to this new situation as an expansion of democratization and industrialization of poetry in America.[4] The spirit transmitted by Allen to future anthologists drives them to use independent criteria and present texts involved in a process of creation that demands new fields and structures. Struggling against habits and modes of imitation he preferred experimentalism, configuring an initial stage that permitted Charles Bernstein to vindicate in the nineties the concept of "the middle," which blurs the distinction between the elitist and populist cultures.[5]

In his introduction to *In the American Tree*, Ron Silliman specifically mentions a selection of poets from different forums (*This*, *Hills*, *Qu*, to name a few), whose primary goal was to work on "the nature of reality, function of language, nature of meaning, shape and value of literature, function of method, relation between writer and reader, critique of reference and normative syntax" (Silliman xix). Silliman seems share Donald M. Allen's intention. It is not so much to create a commonly shared value as to have the cultural privilege of creating a symbiosis between practice and theory, where institutional culture is the nucleus to be reconsidered. The discursive modes presented in the poetics section (after dividing the poets in the poetry section into West and East) entitled "Second Front," clarify the political approach of literature to reality, "by eroding the claim of truth verification in the theory/criticism side of the ledger" (Rasula 405). Of course, Silliman's anthology does not try to cover a historical period as Allen's does but shows a representative poetic formation which was struggling against forms of contention, canonized by former tendencies considered experimental, like the projectivists, and preferred to investigate new methods, "hopefully to renew itself, so that it might offer readers the same opacity, density, otherness, challenge and relevance persons find in the "real" world" (Silliman xvi).

Silliman formalized the language group for the critics in *In the American Tree*, and definitely helped to expand the philosophical premise of "rejecting a speed-based poetics and consciously raising the issue of reference, to suggest that any new direction would require poets to look (in some ways for the first time) at what a poem is actually made of—not images, not voice, not characters or plot, all of which appear on paper, or in one's mouth, only through the invocation of a specific medium, language itself" (Silliman xvi). Silliman's aesthetic choice is clear since it is limited to poets who participated in the l=a=n=g=u=a=g=e project, the sense of affiliation is clearly established. The significant division between East and West is intended to cover the whole country and thus gives the impression that the new proposals were developed throughout the U.S. The introduction written by Silliman and the contributors' notes help to clarify the frameworks around which those poets moved. Moreover, the poetics section was the scale used to enlighten the reader on the innovative epistemology of the creative work.

The poetics section, entitled "Second Front," presents a wide scope ranging from theoretical proposals (Jackson Mac Low, Lyn Hejinian, Steve Benson, Bruce Andrews, Ron Silliman, Charles Bernstein, and Barrett Watten), through suggestive notes (Carla Harryman, Robert Grenier, Ted Greenwald, Nick Piombino), reviews (Tina Darragh, Susan Howe), responses (Rae Armantrout), letters (Clark Coolidge, Kit Robinson), preface

(Stephen Rodefer) or biographical statement conceived as the insight behind her writings (Lynne Dreyer), as far as collaborative essays (Bernadette Mayer and the members of the St. Mark's Church Poetry Project Writing Workshop, and the collection of short essays written by Ron Silliman, Barrett Watten, Steve Benson, Lyn Hejinian, Charles Bernstein, and Bob Perelman, for the magazine *Change*). These diverse approaches develop an intersubjective discourse that cries out for the materiality of the text, breaking down the claims of conventional meanings. Donald M. Allen's poetics section is also diverse, since projectivist, New York School and Beat poets gave voice to different writing approaches, a pluralistic response to modernism by a nonconformist culture. However, Barrett Watten remarks that language poetry has gone further and exceeded these movements, in opposition to Paul Mann's theory-death of the avant-garde, because it has developed "forms of multi-authorship" in some publications that have "united authorship and genre in suprasubjective forms of discourse,"[6] projecting their theories beyond their own generation. This would explain why Silliman's anthology was reprinted in 1999, fourteen years after its first publication, coinciding significantly with Donald M. Allen's second edition of *The New American Poetry*.

Mary M. Sloan's *Moving Borders: Three Decades of Innovative Writing by Women*, also follows Donald M. Allen's and Ron Silliman's inclination in presenting poets writing in innovative forms and including a poetics section. In contrast to Silliman, who prefers to base himself in the aesthetics of one group, Mary M. Sloan focuses on writing developed by women in a historical period. These two anthologies are linked by their narrower scope if compared to Donald M. Allen's, but they differ substantially in their goals while historicizing a period. Sloan collects the poems and poetics written by women only, over three decades, and her selection is not exclusively feminist,[7] and Silliman is just anthologizing a movement. Sloan is more interested in how women poets display the obliteration of boundaries in poetry and how the "radical is always contextual" (Sloan 3). The creative work selected for this anthology covers a wide range from Lorine Niedecker to Melanie Neilson, arranged chronologically according to publication dates. The historicizing viewpoint of this anthology is seen more clearly through the primary work selected by Sloan, since she also, strangely enough, includes Niedecker's poetry, and gives a review of contrastive poetic modes as exemplified by Bernadette Mayer, Anne Waldman, Lyn Hejinian and Julie Patton, to name but a few.

The complementary section "Poetics and Exposition" reinforces that sense of exploration and opposition to Academia, which, as we have seen in Allen's and Silliman's anthologies, became the dominant spirit for compilations of avant-garde poetry in the eighties and nineties. The essays in the complementary section theorize on a poetics which illustrates articulations associated with different trends and individual approaches. As in Silliman's anthology, their poetics is expressed in forms as different as formal essays (Rachel Blau DuPlessis, Rosmarie Waldrop, Lyn Hejinian, Rae Armantrout, Erica Hunt, Carla Harryman, Joan Retallack), letters (Maureen Owen, Dodie Bellamy), evocative notes (Ann Lauterbach, Susan Gervitz, Leslie Scalapino, Beverly Dahlen, Fanny Howe, Tina Darragh, Laura Moriarty), reviews on other poets which reflect their own concerns (Marjorie Welish, Susan Howe, Norma Cole, Kathleen Fraser, Tina Darragh, Cole Swensen), approaches which combine the author's poetry along with poetical thought (Alice Notley), or just use poetry (Bernadette Mayer). In most of them, poetic value has replaced the question of gender and poets are quick to focus on formal innovations, ideological issues or a new *gestalt*. Sloan is successful in charting the emerging women poets as they respond to changing social circumstances in a new cultural debate characterized by heterogeneity applicable to both women and men. In fact, many of the issues and devices discussed in their statements on poetics appear as seminal ideas containing experiences or theoretical formulations akin to their male counterparts: culture, process, representation, voice, syntax, tradition, word, and meaning. All are challenged by imaginative perspectives that give rise to experimental compositions.

The poetics section of *Moving Borders* has been arranged by Sloan "as a conversational sequence...aspect of each selection, whether central or minor, suggests a feature of the one that succeeds it" (Sloan 7). That conversation is typically experimental, since its main goal is based "on the interrogation of forms of representation and on the opening and investigation of literary structures and genres" (Sloan 6). From the first nineteenth-century female anthology in America, Rufus Griswold's *Gems from American Female Poets* (1842), collected within an ethos of moral purity, "propriety and beauty of thought,"[8] up to Sloan's, there has been a long road of discovery. Today's women poets also challenge normative discourse, and their poetics is indistinguishable from men's in questioning representation and cultural practices centered on the textual quality of poetry.

Primary Trouble: An Anthology of Contemporary American Poetry is another variation on Donald M. Allen's anthology. In fact, in the introduction Leonard Schwartz identifies his three main sources: some poets selected earlier in Donald M. Allen's anthology, the New York School and language poetry. His program is inclined towards presenting poetry that evokes a more textual and discursive rather than narrative or lyric experience, focusing on the freshness of a poetics produced in the 1970s, 80s, and 90s. The editors of *Primary Trouble* may be accused of being too pluralistic and ambitious; indeed the criterion of including only the poets born after 1933 is capricious (incidentally, though older poets like William Bronk and Gerrit Lansing appear in the Contributors' Book Publications section, their poetry and poetics are not included). Their main failure is to ignore the poets born after 1950 in the Poetics section. Consequently, the juxtaposition of the Poetry section is not reflected there. In any case, their selection shares the same goal as Allen's, Silliman's and Sloan's anthologies, "to elevate a certain poetics into view against the mainstream poetics that might obscure it."[9] If this is an inaccuracy (we only have poets like Virginia Hooper, Andrew Joron or David Shapiro), it should not be taken to show how vulnerable the editors can be, but as a desire to revise a historical period and, as Alan C. Golding suggests referring to other generic anthologies, probably involving "maintenance and preservation, yes, but also rearticulation, addition and critique" (Golding, "New" 13).

The poets are arranged alphabetically and the selection does not claim to be representative but to offer a poetics that helps us to see "the varieties of perspective as well as the points of intersection" (Schwartz 4). *Primary Trouble*'s poetic range extends from Diane Di Prima and Ted Berrigan to Lee Ann Brown and Drew Gardner, who are the youngest poets in this anthology. They share common terms reminding us of the Silliman's preoccupation with values of poetic language practices, as explained by Leonard Schwartz in his introduction: "these propositions all manifest the urge to go beyond the givens of subjecthood and objecthood, identity and commodity, experience and syntax" (Schwartz 4). Once again, different formal presentations are used for the essays on poetics, coinciding with those found in Silliman's and Sloan's anthologies. Will Alexander chooses the academic essay to express his ideas, Clark Coolidge prefers poetry, Edward Foster, Fanny Howe, Robert Kelly and Gustaf Sobin develop their theories through dispersed notes or reflective thoughts. Leslie Scalapino articulates her aesthetic judgments in an interview and Anne Waldman writes from the interface between her own biography and the poem. This prevailing spirit of fusion produces an amalgam of styles and ideas, which allows us to perceive the continuous evolution of American poetry as well as a dialogue between its creators. Covering a wide range of authors and poetryscapes, the editors show the diversity of recent American poetry, and also sharing the view that what was once disregarded as marginal or too radical is now to be reappraised and marketed.

These three anthologies have common concerns. Firstly, mention should be made of the intellectual play of re-considering the poetry that rebels against academic verse, a paradigm derived from Donald M. Allen's *The New American Poetry*. Being opposed to mainstream poetics not only means rejecting formalism, but also the necessity of formulating a poetics that aligns words and meaning in an adventurous response presenting the innovative poets as iconoclasts. Their only affiliation is experimentalism. Secondly, their selections might be accused of sectarianism. However since many of these editors, particularly Ron Silliman (*Tottel's*) and Edward Foster (*Talisman*) were or are editors of magazines, we should understand that their selections not only derive from their personal tastes but also from the responses received from their various cultural contexts and individuals. These obviously correspond ultimately to the pluralistic society they are immersed in. It does not surprise us that this type of anthology-making is not aimed so much at establishing a new paradigm as at extending continual re-evaluations of poetry,—thereby mixing attitudes, poets and aesthetic choices; framing commitments but also varied suggestions as the necessary stimuli to keep this discipline constantly new. In contrast to Allen, all the editors of the analyzed collections are themselves poets, following the pattern suggested by Robert Duncan, who first dismissed Donald M. Allen's anthology because he was not a poet and could perilously be "teaching or arbitrating the art"[10] rethinking poetry from within and without. Another detail is that all these poets are white, middle class and in some way related to educational institutions. This aspect deserves more extended study but the perceived white authority over other ethnic or cultural minorities reveals the different economic conditions and social status in the politics of avant-garde tendencies.

The climate of avant-garde poetic taste around this fin-de-siècle is presided over by a challenging of the habitual modes of writing and perception, an inevitable pre-condition for further steps in discovering new writing processes. The difference with respect to other periods is that there has been a proliferation of anthologies in recent decades, helping us to more clearly view the rapid changes and short-lived canons. Jed Rasula points out that today's American poetry is configured by four zones: (1) Poetic instruction provided by workshops within the Associated Writing Programs. (2) The New Formalism tendency recuperating traditional metrical forms. (3) The Language Poetry spirit, challenging the possibilities of language itself with its "critical reputation." (4) Groups composed of communities like the women's movement, Afro-American and Chicano trends, which truly deserve the term multiculturalism (Rasula 440). This is a clear sign of the wide acceptance of various poetic commitments made clear by the continued presence of anthologies during the last few decades. If Paul Hoover's *Postmodern American Poetry: A Norton Anthology* (1994), the another anthology of this period that includes a poetics section, has not been touched upon it is because nearly half the poets writing on their own poetics, included by Hoover, already appeared previously in Donald M. Allen's anthology. It being a Norton publication, teaching purposes seem to demand a larger work to represent the latest innovations in American poetry. The three anthologies analyzed here show a more recent view and my position is that when "poetics sections" appear in these anthologies, they help readers to evaluate and reflect upon the construction of a discipline that voices the creative impulse as the dominant feature in this post-industrial society. These new anthologies are not merely teaching tools for lecturers and students. The poetics sections are useful to all readers in perceiving what is "new," what the boundaries of the literary "-isms" are and how the sociological and political aspects of meaning-making become obvious.

NOTES

1. Jonathan Holden takes this assumption from Charles Altieri's *Sense and Sensibility in Contemporary American Poetry*, implying that there has been a shift in poetic authority from poets to critics, a critical discourse which is privileged over poetic discourse. Anthologies which include a section on poetics make it explicitly clear that sensitivity and technical baggage can be best understood from the poets themselves. Jonathan Holden, "American Poetry: 1970-1990," *A Profile of Twentieth-Century American Poetry*, ed. Jack Myers and David Wojahn (Carbondale: Southern Illinois UP, 1991), 270-71.
2. Alan C. Golding suggests that there were two motives behind 19th-century anthologies, "the historicizing and the inspirational," through which to defend the emerging national spirit and the moral purity. Nevertheless for him, "Today preservation usually means selecting from abundance, not protecting from oblivion." But I think that Allen not only confronted the academic establishment by publishing an alternative poetry, but was also conscious of its marginality and potential obliteration. See Alan C. Golding, "A History of American

Poetry Anthologies," *Canons*, ed. Robert von Hallberg (Chicago: U of Chicago P, 1984), 279-307.

3. Alan C. Golding's emphatic point is that Allen was very interested in presenting "new work" rather than "in *historicizing* its precedents," in contrast to anthologists like Paul Hoover, Eliot Weinberger and Douglas Messerli. "New, Newer, and Newest American Poetries," *Chicago Review* 43.4 (Fall 1997): 12. Consequently, of the three anthologies analyzed here, Allen's intention would be followed only by Ron Silliman's *In the American Tree*, which is not only the presentation of a poetic group, but also an "exercise in community development" questioning the internal relationships between writing and the constitution of an audience, as Silliman himself suggests. See Jed Rasula, *The American Poetry Wax Museum: Reality Effects, 1940-1990* (Urbana: National Council of Teachers of English, 1996) 447. I insist that the common goal of the three anthologies analyzed here is to include experimental work as practiced in poetry and theorized in poetics.
4. "...partly because of available funding, but also because of the 'democratized,' *non*literary character of much poetry in the late sixties and early seventies, the institution of the 'poetry reading' flourished on college campuses as perhaps it never had before," Jonathan Holden, *The Fate of American Poetry* (Athens: U of Georgia P, 1991) 21. This democratization means for Holden that "poetry could become a body of knowledge available to people who didn't necessarily read very much or well" (20).
5. Charles Bernstein's main motto, "Just because something is neglected is sufficient reason to consider it," *My Way: Speeches and Poems* (Chicago: U of Chicago P, 1999) 41. Questioning high and low art he praises "the obscure, the peripheral or marginal or minor, the avant-garde, the complex, the eccentric, the dark, the distasteful, the ugly, the inassimilable, the erotic, the repulsive, the formally unsettling" (40-41). Inevitably Bernstein is against normalization and prefers what he terms "signifying practices."
6. Barrett Watten refers explicitly to the collaborative work they have developed since the beginnings of the Language School. Publications like *Legend*, *The Wide Road*, the Language magazines, or collaborative essays like those which appeared in *In the American Tree*, have provided "a powerful analogy to a recent form of avant-garde tendency, the poetics Listserve," "The Secret History of the Equal Sign: *L=a=n=g=u=a=g=e* between Discourse and Text," *Poetics Today* 20.4 (Winter 1999) 623. Barrett Watten understands that in Paul Mann's theory-death, "agency is distributed in institutions, leaving only the negative moment of critique; author and genre disappear into contexts that proscribe any agency." But the Language School continues as an avant-garde tendency because their "suprasubjective forms of discourse," as exhibited in their multi-authored publications, can still be seen in the electronic Poetics List at SUNY Buffalo which

is a "form of intersubjective aesthetic discourse predicated on its radical textuality" (623).

7. Mary M. Sloan emphasizes that "Some of the writers included here identified themselves as feminists, some participated in organized women's writing activities, some focused on issues of gender in their writing. Others did not." Mary Margaret Sloan, introduction, *Moving Borders: Three Decades of Innovative Writing by Women* (Jersey City: Talisman House, 1998), 4-5.

8. In general, the 19th-century American anthologies should be approached with the "conviction that American poetry should be represented by specimens of the utmost moral purity... [and that] delayed the acceptance of any poet who appeared to violate it" (Golding, "History" 288-89). Conversely, heterogeneous and radical approaches as exemplified by the multiple poetic publications in small presses, magazines, and by electronic means have been accepted more easily during these last few decades and consequently been reproduced more rapidly. In this sense, Donald M. Allen's anthology opened the door to the illusion that avant-garde proposals cannot be delayed to reach wider audiences. Marjorie Perloff has also studied this phenomenon, reiterating the popularity of this once alternative poetry shown by the publication of five anthologies, edited by Eliot Weinberger, Paul Hoover, Douglas Messerli, Peter Gizzi and Dennis Barone, "in the two-year span of 1993-94.... A new avant-garde thus seems to be in the making—indeed oxymoronic as it may sound, a new avant-garde consensus." See Marjorie Perloff, "Whose New American Poetry?: Anthologizing in the Nineties," *Diacritics* 26.3-4 (1996), 104-23.

9. Leonard Schwartz, introduction, *Primary Trouble: An Anthology of Contemporary American Poetry*, eds. Leonard Schwartz, Joseph Donahue and Edward Foster (Jersey City: Talisman House, 1996), 3.

10. Initially Robert Duncan objected to *The New American Poetry* because the edition was compiled by a non-poet like Donald M. Allen, but also because "he rejects a venture that he sees as dominated by aspirations toward taste-making, career-building, influence, and representation of a period." See further details in Alan Golding, "*The New American Poetry* Revisited Again," *Contemporary Literature* 39.2 (Summer 1998), 188-89.

WORKS CITED

Allen, Donald M. *The New American Poetry*. New York: Grove, 1960.

Golding, Alan C. "*The New American Poetry* Revisited Again." *Contemporary Literature* 39.2 (Summer 1998): 188-89.

Lazer, Hank. *Opposing Poetries: Issues and Institutions*. Evanston: Northwestern UP, 1996.

Rasula, Jed. *The American Poetry Wax Museum: Reality Effects, 1940-1990*. Urbana: National Council of Teachers of English, 1996.

Schwartz, Leonard. Introduction. *Primary Trouble: An Anthology of Contemporary American Poetry.* Ed. Leonard Schwartz, Joseph Donahue and Edward Foster. Jersey City: Talisman House, 1996.

Silliman, Ron. "Language, Realism, Poetry." *In the American Tree.* Orono: National Poetry Foundation, 1986. xix.

Sloan, Mary Margaret. Introduction. *Moving Borders: Three Decades of Innovative Writing by Women.* Jersey City: Talisman House, 1998.

6

The Power of the Poet and the Power of Word: Emerson and Whitman's Mythologies of Power

VIORICA PATEA

The Poet as Hero

Within the Romantic climate of thought of the nineteenth century, the theories concerning the nature of art and artist are ultimately predicated on conceptions of power. Romanticism conceived of poetry and poet as demiurgic modalities of power. Poetic creation was seen in terms of a power-making act of knowledge, and the Romantic artist, quite often, expressed his will-to-power in almost god-like acts of creation. The Romantic faith led to the hypostatization of art and the subsequent deification of the artist.

If in ancient literature the prototypical hero was primarily a warrior, in the medieval ages a knight or a saint, and in the Renaissance a prince, the most emblematic icon of the Romantic period was the figure of the artist. The artist is Romanticism's most worshipped hero and plays a fundamental part in Romantic thought. The Romantic coronation of the artist was backed by Romantic epistemology that considered imagination and intuition superior modes of knowledge. The Romantic theory of Imagination advanced transcendental claims to the possibility of the poet's achieving absolute knowledge. His art was the outgrowth of his self-empowering vision that articulates the poetics of the Absolute.

Modernity has been prodigious in a whole range of great

heroes, of whom the poet represents the fruits of the nineteenth-century apostlehood of man. The nineteenth century distinguished itself with the creation of Faustian heroes, demigods and supermen, embodiments of the absolute, sovereign, and supreme Self. It was essentially an age of great "Heroes and Hero Worship" in Carlyle's phrase. This cult of man's inner divinity with its subsequent exaltation of the man of genius started with the celebration of the artist as creator.

The figure of the hero artist is a prominent American contribution to the Romantic panoply of towering heroes of the nineteenth century. American Romantics were fascinated by the hero artist motif. They produced a prodigious gallery of artist heroes. Emerson's essays, "The American Scholar" (1837), "Nature," and "The Poet," "Self-Reliance" celebrated the poet as the young nation's founding hero. The poet was also the adopted *poetic persona* of Whitman's speaker in *Leaves of Grass,* who assumed a prophetic demiurgic role. The poet as hero became the prototype of the American superman. He represented the ultimate ideal of self-reliance, self-sufficiency, and freedom. He made the creed of self-reliance and sovereignty the specific idiom of the American sublime. The poet carried out the deification of man, epitome of the sovereign self and paragon of absolute power, whose Faustian ambitions approach the dawn of Nietzsche's Superman. Clinging to the age's dream of man's perfectibility and reformist ardor, Whitman and Emerson presented the most extremely hopeful version of the hero poet: he was a creator, the apotheosis of the man-God who had re-fathomed the universe anew. Moreover, he illustrated the Romantic ideal of man's creative power. Not only did the divinely inspired poet become divine, but he was also the bearer of a new Gospel that made man equal to gods.

The portraits Emerson and Whitman present of their poets map out figures of power: the expression of untrammeled freedom and potentiality. The pose of the poet is that of a dormant demiurge unconscious of the hidden promise he bears within, but gradually taking cognizance of his own concealed power. Stirred out of lethargy, he is a giant who casts off the fetters of his sleep only to rise to the stature of his inner promise.

Emerson's incarnation of the poet as hero is the Orphic poet. His definition of the poet is threefold: he is the representative man, the central man, and the sovereign. Whitman's equivalent of the Emersonian model is the "kosmic" poet, who is "august," "immortal," sometimes even "deathless"[1] (Song 48), invariably illimitable "I...was never measured/and never will be measured" (Song 83), and not to be "contain'd between my hat and my boots" (Song 35).

The nineteenth century harbored faith in the power and will of great men, the men of genius who exert their power over history, forge their own destiny and the fate of nations. Time was made by their designs. Nations surged from their volition. These were the Napoleons, Byrons, Fausts and Ahabs. And in America, the nation was to be founded by poets. American Romantics saw in the poet the powerful founding hero of a great nation and a new man who was to redeem mankind. The poet as hero is the outgrowth of a worldview in which history is forged by the free will of extraordinary men. Whitman's regal imperative "Produce great Persons, the rest follows" (By Blue 342) sums up the prevailing confidence in the cult of the exceptional man.

Emerson hailed the poet as a sort of demiurge; his arrival was comparable to the advent of a God who marked the beginning of a new era, "the principal event in chronology"[2] (DSA 987). America needed its founding hero, since the fortunes and bounties of the promised land "are yet unsung" (Poet 997). Emerson depicted the new continent pining for the arrival of its long awaited hero: "time and bravery yield us many gifts, but not yet the timely man, the new religion, the reconciler, whom all things await" (Poet 997). Like a lover, the new continent pined for the arrival of its awaited hero. In response, Whitman presented himself as the continent's poet-prophet Emerson anticipated. He took up Emerson's exhortation, reformulating it as an overbearing challenge addressed to him by a pseudo Shakesperean phantom, no longer exacting vengeance but imperious action "demanding bards,/By them all native and grand, by them alone can these States be fused into the compact organism of a Nation" (By Blue 346). Whitman's "kosmic" bard is fashioned upon Emersonian high expectations. His "poets to come" (LG 14) chant the creation of a new race "the race of races" (Preface 1855, 713), "a race dominating previous ones and greater far" (Starting 27).

The Poet and the Word

Emerson and Whitman placed heroic demands on the poet. As Bloom observes, he was meant to be "a new Adam, new Moses, a new Christ" (177). The poet as hero emerged in the wake of the decline of the gods and any other supernatural beings above him. At the dawn of modernity, God became a *deus absconditus,* no longer present in the world, experienced mainly as an intolerable void. In his absence, the Romantic poet stepped out into the silence of empty spaces in an effort to bridge the intervening hiatus between gods and man. He tried to mend the discontinuous, fragmentary and alienating condition of the world and restore its old harmonies anchored in the certitude of God's presence. His poetic vision was the assertion of a will that tried to breach the gap between heaven and earth and fill the void with his own imaginary worlds.

As Hillis Miller observes, the Romantic poet is "a new type of man…who in absence of a given world must create his own" (14). Once the heavens remain silent, he ceases to be a prophet receiving revelation, and becomes a prophet god himself, no longer a vehicle of a power descending upon him from above, but a champion of his own creative power. His imaginative narratologies are the fruit of his own alternative, autonomous revelation.

Finally, the poet is a prophet in quest of the divine one who attempts to bring God back to earth as a power inherent in man and exemplifies his newly reached faith by embodying it himself. He blurs the difference between the sacred and the profane, by assuming the sacred and eventually delivering it into the self. The poet defies God's absence with his own creative powers, the fabric of new representations, symbols, and fictions. The Emersonian poet speaks as a demiurge emancipated from everyman's condition of bondage. No longer "a God in ruins" (Nature 929), but, unlike others, unchained, he metes out his Promethean fire. Man is not a simple channel or vehicle of the deity, but its tenor "for we are not pans and barrows, nor even porters of the fire and torchbearers, but children of the fire, made of it, and only the same divinity transmuted" (Poet 985). Meanwhile, Whitman's bard complains that except for him "none has begun to think how divine he himself is" (Starting 20).

The Romantic poet was committed to the "model of the writer as prophet and literature as Scripture" (Buell 1987: 184). He embarked on the quest for a new scripture. The power of his poetic word was that of a new Gospel. Emerson declared the Bible an open text and reduced religion to a form of poetic inspiration. The prophet's inspired vision is not different in nature from the artist's poetic inspiration. Both are different forms of poesis. Emerson remarked that "the religions of the world are the ejaculations of a few imaginative men" (Poet 996). His Logos acquired a specifically idiosyncratic and iconoclastic meaning, and consciousness became a power in itself since any "thought may be ejaculated as Logos, or Word" (Poet 998). Emerson exhorted every man to become a poet, conscious that it is within his power to become "a newborn bard of the Holy Ghost...and acquaint men at firsthand with the deity" (DSA 954). The poet became the exemplary model of man's emancipation. In response to Emerson's call, Whitman attempted to flesh out the Emersonian program of intellective independence. His answer was a cry of faith: "I too...inaugurate a new religion" (Starting 20) and he presented himself as the Moses and Christ of a new religion destined to write the "evangel-poem of comrades and love" (Starting 19) of the New World.

Literary scripturism was a popular mode of writing, emblematic of the nineteenth century, that spread the prevailing "idea of the writer as prophet commissioned to write the ultimate scripture-poem of the universe" (Buell 1987, 182). Hence, the attempt of so many Romantic writers such as Blake and Carlyle, Schiller and Goethe, Emerson and Whitman to create new religions, mythologies, cosmologies, and scripts of modernity in which the world and its entire frame of reference is refashioned, and made anew.

In his essay "On Goethe," Emerson urged: "we too must write Bibles, to unite again the heavens and the earthly world."[3] Emerson proposed Romantic books that present an "original relation to the universe" (Nature 903). Whitman conceived of *Leaves of Grass* as the scriptures of modernity and his poetic persona ardently adopted the role of a self-appointed messiah to the point of inducing many of his earlier admirers and critics to hail him as a new Buddha or Christ (Bucke 1:1, 9:6; LG 562).

The man-God was the visceral, closeted temptation of the nineteenth century. As Norman Mailer observes, America is the land "where a new kind of man was born from the idea that God was present in every man not only as compassion but as power" (288). Once the poet is conceived as God, he is redefined in terms of power and will. By containing a spark of God man becomes God, in a process in which the fragment is elevated to an encompassing whole. The soul inhabited by the Supreme Spirit becomes the expression of its sovereignty. Emerson asked, "who can set bounds to the possibilities of man? Once...man has access to the entire mind of the Creator, is himself the creator in the finite" (Nature 926).

Emerson's frequent formulations of the poet as hero are expressions of power: the Orphic Poet "rests upon the bosom of God: he is nourished by unfailing fountains, and draws... inexhaustible power" (Nature 926). To Emerson "the poet is the person in whom these powers are in balance, the man without impediment" (Poet 985). Absolute master of his fate, his will alone determines his destiny in a display of omnipotence that finds no barriers. The poet is a creator born out of the idea of an indwelling divinity, celebrated as the manifestation of the will and power of the self, which renders him utterly self-subsistent and self-reliant.

The notion of man as power is a corollary of the notion of God as power. Emerson's ground of being, the ultimate *quidditas*, is a refashioning of the aprioristic Platonic principle into, essentially, a manifestation of power: "the highest is present to the soul of man...the dread universal essence, which is not wisdom, or love or beauty, or power, but all in one, and each entirely, is that of which all things exist, and that by which they are" (Nature 926). Even the moral sentiment, Emerson's "law of laws" (DSA 946) is a form of power. It purports to "the beatitude of man" (DSA 946), a euphoria that underscores his illimitability.

The supreme expression of power is to be found in the role of the poet as God. The divine is the utmost modality of power and to the extent to which the poet, and indirectly man for that matter, appropriates it he becomes a man-God. As such, the poet has complete sway over his own fate, and by extension over the larger destiny of mankind.

Whitman's equivalent for the Emersonian Orphic poet is the "kosmic poet," another apostle of man's divinity. The "kosmic" poet realizes Emerson's ideal of self-sufficiency and self-reliance. He is the maker of his own conditions. He himself is an allegory of supreme power—"I troop forth replenish'd with supreme power, one of the average unending procession" (Song 72); he also becomes a god, but a god greater than gods, just as he is a "kosmos" larger than the cosmos.

Both Kosmic and Orphic poets are ultimately poet-gods. However, they represent the power of the common man, and their origin is that of the low. Thus, Emerson avows: "I embrace the common, I explore and sit at the feet of the familiar, the low" (AS 942), and Whitman declares, "the genius of the United States is...in the common people" (LG 712). Yet, the power of the common man rests on strange godlike underpinnings. Whitman's hero poet will represent the "divine average" (Starting 21). Although the kosmic poet is endowed with superhuman characteristics, his power is the power of the lowly, the humble, the voiceless, the defeated and the slave, full of Christ-like overtones. He will praise the excellence of the unholy, the exceptionality of the rough, the pre-eminence of the inferior. The hero-poet brings forth the aggrandizement of the common man and elevates him to the highest peak of power. He is the apotheosis of the self, "a simple separate person" ("Inscriptions" 1), elevated to godlike stature.

The Orphic and the "Kosmic" Poet

The model Emerson chose for his redeemer and savior national poet was that of the Orphic bard. There is a striking similitude between Emerson's "Orphic poet" and Orphism. Orphic poems contained a *hieroi logoi* and constituted a sacred literature, which placed high importance on the salvation of the individual soul through initiation, just as Emerson presented his own Orphic fragments as a higher revelation "ejaculated as Logos" (Poet 998) for the redemption of the individual self. The Orphics ran counter to the prevailing conception of religion as an outward duty to the state and redefined it as a craving for salvation of the individual soul. They opposed institutionalized religion and its formal rituals in favor of a conception of religion that was basically an experience of the soul, just as Emerson was to rebel against historical Christianity and "show us that God is, not was; that he speaketh, not spake" (DSA 953), or Whitman was to keep "creeds and schools in abeyance" (Song 29).

Emerson's approach is as subversive as the Orphic belief. He also taught religious experience as an individual act of the soul, disdained the formalists of the pulpit and urged to "love God without mediator or veil" (DSA 953). The Orphics disregarded ideas of clan and state and emphasized the existing relationship between the One and the many, the human and the divine and their potential unity. They harbored the promise of man's immortality. The Orphics preached the divinity of the human soul and urged men to cast away all other ties that prevent the emergence of their divine and immortal nature. Their object was to save the soul by a life of moral uprightness in the final hope of becoming one with the divine.

Between Emerson's awareness that "poets are liberating Gods. They are free and they make free" (Poet 995) and the exultant cry of the devotee who reached the awareness "God am I, mortal no longer" (Guthrie 327) the difference is slight. Emerson's Orphic poet is also the prophet of man's divinity. He, too, promotes man's complete independence in the name of a "divine and deifying" (DSA 946) power in his own soul that "makes him illimitable" (DSA 946). He evangelizes the dogma of God within. His secret sacred doctrine rests on "the infinitude of man" (DSA 953). As a prophet, Emerson's Orphic poet decries man's present lamentable condition, "a god in ruins"

(Nature 929), oblivious of his own immortality. His mission is to shake the self out of forgetfulness and restore it to the awareness of its hidden transcendental identity.

Emerson's poet "stands among partial men for the complete man" (Poet 985). The Emersonian Orphic reintroduces the idea of man's original wholeness, a wholeness of origins that imply the fundamental unity between the human and the divine. He himself embodies this sense of entirety. The poet is the man who "reattaches things to nature and the Whole" (Poet 990). He redresses the fundamental hiatus that lies at the core of Being by correcting the present "dislocation and detachment from the life of God" (Poet 990). He is the bearer of a secret knowledge of occult origins and a lost primordial unity.

Emerson's story is the story of a God who has forgotten his high origin and who is restored to his true power. The poet is the first Titan to have awakened from his long sleep of Reason. His newly gained understanding turns him into the prophet of the apologetics of man. His narratives are primarily mythologies of man and his original greatness, "Once man was all: now he is an appendage, a nuisance" (DSA 947). The Orphic poet's leitmotif is a lamentation, "man is the dwarf of himself" (Nature 929), the subtext of which is a celebration of man as god and power. His role as prophet is to evoke this mnemonic recollection of man as God, but in the modern myth, memory is replaced by self-awareness and self-consciousness marks the onset of the empowering process. The prophetic efforts of the poet consist in inducing this higher form of self-awareness. Emerson's Orphic fiction is the apologue of the lost unity with the godhead within himself. He tells the story of man's present destitution. Man is a manifestation of the divine, but because he has lost awareness of his true condition at present he is a mere fragment.

Whitman's version of Emerson's Orphic poet is the "kosmic poet" whose incarnation he believes himself to be. The "kosmos" is the trope for the self's creative power in incessant expansion, an allegory of the abundance of his own creation. The poet's "kosmic" attributes underscore his infinitude, "this incredible God I am" (Song at Sunset 495).

If Emerson saw in the poet a liberating god, Whitman saw in him a *summum* of worlds. His songs affirm the belief that "the spirit of God is the brother of my own" (Song 45). As a prophet god he also preaches the divine condition of man: "Is it wonderful that I should be immortal? As everyone is immortal" (LG 394). He set out to "wash the gum of your eyes" (Song 84) and compelled every man to become one of these "Supreme Gods," to grow into "one of the supremes" (Song 76). He argued that the self can realize his inner divinity and set himself as proof and exemplifying model: "divine I am inside and out, and I make holy whatever I touch or am touch'd from" (Song 53). Once the poet became aware of this power within himself he became first its vehicle and then its incarnation.

Emerson's Orphic poet as later Whitman's kosmic poet apportions divine power to men. The two exemplify how to become a creator, and becoming a creator signifies becoming a god. Both democratize the divine and mete out the prerogatives of power entailed by the divine. In "The Divinity School Address" Emerson censured the fallacy according to which "the divine nature is attributed to one or two persons, and denied to all the rest" (DSA 947). Emerson's prophetic paradigm is Christ, but a Christ transformed into the bearer of a utopian message, not God's gospel but that of man's greatness, which recognizes man as God (DSA 947). He pleads for "the divine idea which each of us represents" (Self-Reliance 957). Neither the Orphic nor the "kosmic" poet are exclusive usurpers of power. Whitman's democratic spirit forbids him to claim "nothing to myself which I have not carefully claim'd for others on the same terms" (By Blue 351). He solves the problem of supreme authority by positing not only one Supreme, but various Supremes and, hence, by infusing all with his newly gained self-awareness of the divine.

> Have you thought there could be but a single supreme?
> There can be any number of supremes (By Blue 341).

It is in the person of the poet that the incarnation of the divine gains full cognizance of itself: "All the rest behold in the hero of the poet their own green and crude being—ripened" (AS 940).

Orphic and Kosmic Cosmologies: Mythologies of Power

Nature, Emerson's central philosophical treatise in which he elaborates the myth of the Orphic poet, is a theorization of nature, an ontological account of man and the world, that sets the basis of a new mythos. Emerson's cosmogony contains the most extravagant claims of all on behalf of man. In "Nature" Emerson's Orphic fragments account for the origin of nature and the creation of man. In Emerson's myth the universe is made from the body of an original divinity which, according to his cosmogonic formula, is man. Man and universe share the same spiritual consubstantiality. Out of his body, a kind of spiritual undifferentiated totality, proceed the orbs and the world.

Man is the dwarf of himself. Once he was permeated and dissolved by spirit. He filled nature with his overflowing currents. Out of him sprang the sun and the moon; from man the sun; from woman the moon. The laws of the mind, periods of his actions externalized themselves into day and night, into the year and the seasons. But having made for him this huge shell, his waters retired; he no longer fills the veins and the veinlets; he is shrunk to a drop.... Now man is the follower of the sun, and woman the follower of the moon (Nature 929).

Most myths that narrate the making of the world attribute the authorship to a God who creates it only to disappear later. The ensuing period is usually a fall from the primal unity of the Golden Age. Emerson changes the signification and meaning of the mythic tale: in his account, man and nature start out as creations and emanations of the Universal Spirit. Only midway, Emerson locates the divine in the soul, a process in the course of which the individual self subsumes its ultimate power, and merges in this union with God as the encompasser of the deity, who actualizes in the ground of his being its superhuman birthright. Thus, in Emerson's confabulation "spirit does not act upon us from without, that is in space and time, but spiritually, or through ourselves. Therefore, that spirit—the Supreme Being—does not build up nature around us, but puts it forth through us" (Nature 926). The original union is mystified into a new incarnation, by which the self arrogates the power of origination and integrates his antecedent in a fusion in which the identifying distinctions between the two disappear. Emerson identifies man with spirit and further with the Universal Spirit. Once the creation is completed in this new Genesis, it is no longer God who vanishes to the great chagrin of created beings, but man, his homologue, "who shrunk to a drop." Consequently, man's quest for God becomes man's quest for himself.

According to Emerson Man, not god, constitutes the origin of man and of the phenomenal world. Nature does not represent God's creation later consigned to man for his dominion. Nature is not entrusted to man, but emanates from him. In Emerson, as later in Whitman, cosmogony is not cosmo-centric but anthropocentric, the center of gravity being transferred to man. The objective world is the creation of the subject, while the subject, traditionally the creation of God, reaches the awareness of being actually a god himself. God arrives at self-consciousness in man, an idea with strong Hegelian underpinnings.

In the new myth, the Platonic idealistic worldview which "sees the world in God" (Nature 924) proves insufficient because "it leaves God out of me" (Nature 925), and precludes the "Me" as absolute creator. Idealism sees the world as the fruit of a noumenal reality from which its roots derive. Emerson counters traditional idealistic categories by his spiritualist postulations. The Platonic argument is counterpoised by a new cosmogony in which man assumes the central role. He is the true creator of the world and from him proceeds the created order. From him spring the orbs "sun and moon," and time "day and night," "the year and the seasons" are aspects of his thought, too. The universe is no longer a modality of the absolute, but of man.

Emerson's cosmogony is possible because his epistemological paradigm integrates the One and the many in the belief that the created order proceeds from a universal principle inherent in self and nature. In his own myth of nature and man, he espouses a narration that sees the world as the manifestation of one essence and whose axioms postulate the equivalence of nature and spirit. The manifold variety of the world is but a multiform manifestation of one primordial essence.

Whitman's myth is based on Emerson's monistic, immanent account of man and the world. To him, nature will remain a mysteriously encoded cipher, in which the poet discovers his own and the world's inner divinity. In the Whitmanian fable, nature too is the poet's identity model and allegory of his own immortality. Precisely because he is "kosmic" the "kosmic" poet is bound to find in nature the key to his own identity. In "Song of Myself," the poet descends to the grass roots only to become reacquainted with God and the hidden image he bears engraved within him.

Emerson's metaphysics posit the underlying "unity in variety," a principle which constitutes the universal law of his imaginary universe, according to which "each creature is only a modification of the other...their radical law is one and the same" (Nature 918). Whitman's poetic speaker takes up the same "law." Natural elements bear witness to the one and the same immanent power which lies at the foundation of existence: "they bring me tokens of myself/ They evince them plainly in their possession" (Song 60), and he avows that he "see[s] in them and myself the same old law" (Song 41).

In Emerson and Whitman's myth, nature functions as a metaphor of immortality that reveals the inherent divinity, the world and self. Nature fosters a strong sense of the kosmic poet's inner power, who "hear[s] and behold[s] God in every object" (Song 86). In the very depths of his being he discovers the promise of his infinite becoming: "I see something of God each hour [...]/In the faces of men and women I see God, and in my own face in the glass" (Song 86, 87).

Emerson's equation between spirit and nature, man and god constitutes Whitman's paradigm. Man and God form a tandem. Man in the process of becoming the mouthpiece of the divine merges with it. They are easily interchangeable terms, tenors that elucidate each other reciprocally and encode within themselves the meaning of their correlatives. Their analogous and generic ciphers establish a system of communicating vessels, conduits of sequences of reciprocal transpositions and transfigurations. From this conceptual equation derive other binomers—body and soul, mortality and immortality—that duplicate the Emersonian equation between self and nature and reflect the same monistic tendency to reduce everything to an interchangeable selfsame unitary principle.

The Poet as the World's Center

In Emerson's cosmogonic formula, the world is made out of the substance of divinity that is man. Sun and moon spring from his body, and the world is consubstantial with his spiritual primordiality. Emerson's apologue sees man as an original deity, the maker and origin of the world. The Orphic poet is situated at the origins of time; he begins a new cycle. In Whitman's cosmologic account, the accent falls on the zenith of the evolutionary process. The kosmic poet is the outcome of a millenary process of gestation of an immanent and transcendent principle, unfolding from the "huge first Nothing" (Song 81) and attaining its culmination in man, the demiurge. His ascent from lower inorganic forms to higher levels of awareness marks the incarnation of the spirit in time.

> I am an acme of things accomplish'd, and I an encloser of things to be.
> My feet strike an apex of the apices of the stairs (Song 80, 81).

The kosmic poet becomes the meaning and goal of evolution, he is history's most cherished prophecy. His spiraling upwards through matter places him at the apex of the evolutionary process and sanctions his power as godlike.[4]

Emerson's myth describes the poet as "central." The Orphic poet represents the center, the *fons et origo* of creation, and the first cause from which the world originates. The idea of the poet's centrality is linked to his implicit sovereignty. Thus, the poet is "a sovereign and stands on the centre" (Poet 986). In Whitman's mythical figurations the "kosmic" poet is also central. He is the one invisible seed that inheres in all people: "In all people I see myself none more and not one barley-corn less" (Song 47). Whitman's version of the center is that of an overabundant monad, a fount of self-sufficient selfhood, an excessive welter of overflowing, uncontained divinity, propagating its waves out of the fold to the end of Time. The poet is the inordinate consciousness fleshing out this matrix and indiscriminately bestowing his divine plenitude on the created world. From this center the divine essence is shared and spread through successive circles, which generate in their expansion greater circles, infinitudes within other infinitudes, tautological perspectives of soul and body, in which each is translated in terms of the other, and both become variations on the same reality, following the Emersonian pattern.

In Whitman's cosmology, the world-making poet becomes God, the creator; a self-created man-God who fashions the world anew out of his own unlimited self: "On women fit for conception I start bigger and nimbler babes,/This day I am jetting the stuff of far more arrogant republics" (Song 74). The world is again parented. This time it is the poet's offspring. He spawns an infinitude of possible fictionalized worlds out of himself, a whole new range of created orders, endless possibilities existing outside time, which expand, contain, and at times pre-empt the given order within "becoming already a creator,/Putting myself here and now to the ambush'd womb of the shadow" (Song 76). The poet celebrates his own vital procreative role while he tramps in his open ended journey along the open road which brings the world into being.

Fall and Apotheosis: the Opake and the Transparent

Even though Emerson's cosmogony consecrates the poet's final apotheosis it tells the story of a fall. However, though his fable contemplates the possibility of the fall, it excludes the possibility of evil. Emerson pronounces "all evil is so much death or nonentity" (DSA 946); similarly, Whitman also rejects its conceptual eventuality as an insult to the human being "and I say there is in fact no evil" (Starting 19). Notwithstanding, the fall does not affect the powerful poet, but the world. To Emerson, the fallen world is a world that remains opaque. He explains that once man began to shrink, nature formed a vast solid shell surrounding him: "The axis of vision is not coincident with the axis of things, and so they appear not transparent but opake" (Nature 930). The opaque world remains obdurate, impenetrable and impermeable to the power of spirit.

To render the world whole again, means to render it

transparent. This is in the power of the great man, the great hero. "Wherever a man comes," Emerson says, "there comes revolution...when a man comes all books are legible, all things transparent, all religions are forms" (DSA 953). Transparency is the hallmark of the poet, a further expression of his power of vision, "the poet turns the world to glass, and shows us all things in their right series and procession" (Poet 991). To make the world transparent means to annul the ballast of time and the deadness of perception that have rendered it "opake" and ossified. Transparency is the Emersonian expression of the sublime and the attribute of the poet who brings about the transmutation of the world. A sublimity that sees the world in its initial unity and wholeness, suffused by the currents of the Universal Being. Furthermore, transparency is a form of transcendence that rescues the world from its inflexibility and restores it to its inherent immanence. It is an act of repossession of the word's own "uncontained and immortal beauty" (Nature 905). Its corollary is verticality, the ascent to a higher mode of being, and attainment of sovereignty.

The poet's life-giving power "puts eyes, and a tongue, into every dumb and inanimate object" (Poet 991), absolves the world of its lifeless disjointed condition and restores its vital force. Transparency is predicated upon fluidity. Its mode is not a timeless, immutable clarity, but a life infusing power that destroys the stagnancy of things, and reinserts the world in the streams of the Supreme Spirit, where it becomes "part and particle of God" (Nature 905). The coincidence between the axis of vision and the axis of things does not elicit inalterable categories of truth. Furthermore, truth is not static, but is to be found in endless growth. Truth does not express itself any longer in rigid permanent antinomies as good and evil, but in terms of a dynamic newness, a transparent, dynamic, evolutionary metamorphosis. No longer steadfast, immovable, transfixed in clear-cut blocks of ice, it is conceived of as an electric fluid, a flowing empirical power. To effect the transparency of the world, and make it free and fluid, the poet has to unlock the locked world. It is again the poet who "unlocks our chains, and admits us to a new scene" (Poet 995) and leads to the "brink of waters of life and truth" (Poet 995). To "unlock" presupposes to unleash the immortal constitutive power that can no longer be immured within.

The Poetic Genesis

The Emersonian fable depicts the poet as a prophet restoring the gospel of man's divine self-consciousness. In Whitman, the accent falls on the process of creation itself and on the world as the fruit of his own making. With the "kosmic" poet we actually protagonize a second genesis.

Emerson conceived the poet in terms of a new trinity. He translated the Christian trinitarian principle "the father, the spirit, and the son" into "the Knower, the Doer and the Sayer" (Poet 986), the poet being "the sayer, the namer,...represents beauty" (Poet 986). Emerson's poet, and Whitman's too, speak out of the Biblical belief in a foundational spiritual substance of the created order. "The poet is a Namer, or Language-maker" (Poet 991), the true son of God. It is this power of naming which makes the poet a godlike creator, for language-making is world-making. Emerson argued that "Words and deeds are quite indifferent modes of the divine energy. Words are also actions, and actions are a kind of words" (Poet 986). To name means to create, "the condition of true naming, on the poet's part, is his resigning himself to the divine *aura* which breathes through all forms" (Poet 993). And he who creates becomes in turn a creator, "the sacredness which attaches to the act of creation... is instantly transferred to the record. The poet chanting, was felt to be a divine man" (AS 934). As co-author of a second Genesis, the poet is invested with the ultimate prerogatives of the creator. In the wake of modernity, the poet becomes the prototype of the modern God.

To Emerson, poetic creation constitutes the outburst of an uncontainable power in a new act of rehearsal of the original making of the world—"rage drew out of thee that dream-power...a power transcending all limits and privacy, and by virtue of which a man is the conductor of the whole river of electricity.... Comes he to that power, his genius is no longer exhaustible" (Poet 998). Creation is a re-creation, a second Genesis in which a new world is born again out of the poet's consciousness, Emerson's "Noah's ark," into which the visible world is re-absorbed as into a self-renewing creative matrix and out of which it proceeds, regenerated on a higher plane of being. "All the creatures by pairs and tribes," says Emerson, "pour into his mind as into Noah's ark, to come forth again to people a new world" (Poet 998). But this time, the poet is no longer tied to forms of anteriority. The Orphic poet's mandate is, "Build, therefore your own world" (Nature 931).

Emerson breaks the Christian and Neoplatonic framework: idealism is preempted by "spiritualism." The poet is no longer ancillary of the Absolute, nor art a copy of eternal forms nor the artist their translator. He is no longer an imitator, but a discoverer of the new. In the nineteenth century newness was a source of power. The poet's function is not contingent on the godhead any more nor derived from any pre-existing structures, but paramount. He fully assumes his predominant ascendancy. His creation is a display and exercise of an independent power that fashions its own ontological structures anew.

Whitman appropriates Emerson's prolegomena on the poet's creative power as the conceptual scaffolding of his own work. The poet's creative power is that of naming. If the American poet's stigma is his belatedness, for once, he absolves himself of his *Nachträglichkeit* in this new creation, whose protagonist and architect he is. When he arrives, the world is already there, waiting. Though formed, it lies inert, blind, still shrouded in an atmosphere of chaotic indistinctness waiting for the poet to come in order to receive from him its supreme culmination. Although the world is made, it lingers on inactive. The poet rouses the continent out of torpor. He sees it, and seeing means naming, bringing into being. The world does not really exist in the true sense of the word, until the poet names it anew. As a re-creator he has to name it all, to draw a complete index of the world, since each and every single element of it, from the pismire to the celestial orbs, has to be activated, stirred out of unconsciousness into new life.

The poet is responsible for this new register, which has to be as inclusive as possible as it represents the heritage of the new creation: his index lists constitute the treasure salvaged in

Noah's ark, the Emersonian metaphor of the poet's consciousness, which are to be the seeds of a new creation. Hence, the long lists of catalogues which Emerson prescribes and which Whitman executes are an attempt to circumscribe the world's potential.

The catalogue shows the poet as world-maker. The poet's power of creation and shaping action are manifested in his prodigious lists, the most suitable formal technique to enact his own creation of the world. These lists and catalogues attempt to encompass the totality of the world. Because the catalogue includes, rather than excludes, it is the formal device which reflects the "kosmic" attributes of the poet. Through it the poet strives to attain the absolute wholeness of the world; as he avows: "I reject none, accept all, then reproduce all in my own forms" (By Blue 340).

To create means to name, to bring into existence. The poet has to name the whole world, each and all, every single element of it. The main ambition of Whitman's poetic program is this exhaustive enumeration of the world's register. As Buell[5] has shown, the catalogue is the aesthetic expression of the main tenets of transcendentalism, of a conception rooted in the belief of the existence of a universal spiritual essence inherent in all things and beings which leads to the existence of an underlying unity of "one and all." Thus, Whitman populates and shapes America with a million names and multitudes. There is in Whitman a thirst to name, to call things into being, to give form and shape out of nothingness, and a godlike pleasure in fashioning the non-identified, amorphous, indistinct formlessness into material, fleshy entities. Whitman's creation has a primarily sensual reality, it is not known abstractly, but is meant to be touched, gauged and measured by all the senses.

Naming is a gratuitous act of creation, a relishing of their materiality, a gesture of curious desire to delve into their innermost secret. To name is to bring about a new birth delivered not from the womb of nature but from his own consciousness; the poet's ego expands with every single act of creation. Whitman's sweeping enumerations, strange bazars, bric-a-brac of the spiritual and the material piled-up indiscriminately together, attest to the poet's godlike, self-begetting power. He becomes the supreme expression of the inexhaustible cosmic power that he comes to represent. Naming is the poet's way of quickening the revivifying energy of nature with the power of his word—"I moisten the roots of all that has grown" (Song 50). In Whitman, more overtly than in Emerson, sexual consummation and poetic utterance are correlates. The climactic cry of sexual arousal, "unclench your floodgates, you are too much for me" (Song 58), constitutes the release of the poetic Logos—"I am afoot with my vision" (Song 61).

To know, to name, is to possess. In order to prove himself a true creator, Whitman's strategy is to embrace the whole universe and take possession of it through a process of identification. He acknowledges every single element of it, welcomes it and reveals its splendor and variety. He accepts everything unconditionally from high to low, and ordure to glory, and absorbs it into himself. Whitman pervades everything, becomes everything, admits of no limitations: "I have the idea of all, and am all and believe in all" (With Antecedents 240). Hence, these sprawling lists are assertions of the poet's plenitude and of his omnivorous ego. They underscore the vital energy of the cosmos and of its encompasser, the "kosmic" bard.

At a deeper psychological level, the surfeit of catalogues defeats the existential *angst* of nothingness. The display of such infinite variety, the accretion of multiplicity keep the threat of emptiness at bay. Creation placates the medusa figure of the void. In virtue of their materiality, the accumulation of things and beings vanquish the danger of nonbeing and annul the sense of absence.

Gradually, Whitman's "kosmic" poet grows to the stature of his and the world's own maker. He will finally breed the whole race and continent out of himself, take pleasure and pride in his own making, and, like a second God, will find it good. The poet epitomizes the maker who substantiates the world he has brought into being. He interiorizes it all into himself "all this I swallow, it tastes good, I like it well, it becomes mine" (Song 66). He shapes the all and encompasses it and takes everything in, "Within me latitude widens, longitude lengthens,/Asia, Africa,

Europe..." (Song 138). He embraces everything and possesses all he embraces: "I have embraced you and henceforth possess you to myself" (Song 74). Possessions in Whitman give rise to a long series of identifications, in the course of which he reveals himself as the universal principle that dwells in all people. He observes everything and *is* everything: "I am possessed!/Embody all presences outlaw'd or suffering" (Song 71).

The poet who "observes," "sees," "was there" and "suffers" is the epitome of all he has seen, observed and suffered. He becomes a God, quintessence of the creation he has engendered by naming it: "Askers embody themselves in me and I am embodied in them" (Song 72). Finally, the poet proves himself a Kosmos—he is everywhere and nowhere, "rejecting none, permitting it all" (Song 351).

Whitman's catalogues seem to corroborate Goethe's dictum that everything that enlarges the self is true. This is the privilege of the poet, who empowers himself to create. Schiller pleaded for nature's right to enlarge nature in the bosom of nature, a power he deemed congenial to the man of genius. The poet is the prototype of this exceptional man who becomes co-author of creation. He is endowed with superhuman powers. The kosmic poet's actions are God's actions. After having created nature, he instills life. His breath, like the breath of God, is a power-infusing life spirit—"I do not ask who you are, that is not important to me,/You can do nothing and be nothing but what I will infold you" (Song 74). He also operates the resurrection of the dead, "I dilate you with tremendous breath, I buoy you up/ ...Lovers of me, bafflers of graves" (Song 74).

The Poet as Supreme God: The God among Gods

Yet Whitman's poet emerges as a God among gods. He looms as God's potential rival and finally his vanquisher. His first act is an act of rebellion: he threatens God in his supreme position and usurps his role just as he had usurped his creation before by refashioning it.

Magnifying and applying come I,
Outbidding at the start the old cautious hucksters,

> Taking myself the exact dimensions of Jehovah
> Lithographing Kronos, Zeus, his son, and Hercules his grandson,
> Buying drafts of Osiris, Isis, Belus, Brahma, Buddha,
> In my portfolio placing Manito loose, Allah on a leaf... (Song 75).

Even among gods, the poet ratifies his preeminence. As a new god he is to cast out the gods of the past, "the old signifiers" (Salut au Monde 142) and "cautious hucksters." They no longer constitute the first cause, the primary role in a cosmography. The former gods only serve to pave the way for the Poet to come: "they bore mites as for unfledg'd birds who have now to rise and fly and sing for themselves" (Song 75). Patronizingly, he recognizes their subsidiary value: "taking them all for what they are and not a cent more/Admitting they were alive and did the work of their days" (Song 75). The poet treats the preceding deities as if they were idols, limited, ossified concepts, no longer living gods, but things, emptied of an inner experiential life-meaning substance. As idols they represent what Erich Fromm would call "the alienated manifestation of man's own powers" (Fromm 46). To the "kosmic poet" the former deities incarnate mere convenient stages in man's process of enlightenment. At a time when man was so blind as not to recognize his own powers, they served as an outward screen onto which to project human attributes. With the advent of the Kosmic poet, the old gods can be discarded, for the poet usurps their power and devolves it back to the self. The poet measures himself against the divine outlines of former deities, now hollow husks of "old cautious hucksters," only to fill the old forms with a new living substance and meaning: his own.

> Accepting the rough deific sketches to fill out better in myself,
> Bestowing them freely on each man and woman I see (Song 75).

The poet prophet announces a new dispensation. He announces that "nothing, not God, is greater to one than one's self is" (Song 86). The "old hucksters" are "cautious." The bond with past deities presupposes a hindrance to man's full development because, although they free man from the dominion of man they still demand obedience to their authority. The old gods demand submission, while the poet promises complete independence. They represent the outward form; the poet the inward live meaning.

The poet is a man-God, no longer a God-man. He institutes a new covenant, according to which men and women are divine and will eventually be gods. In the *Genesis*, God made man "in his own image" (*Genesis* 1: 27). Yet, the Biblical God is far too moderate in his promise. Whitman's poet aspires to fulfill an older promise, "ye shall be as gods" (*Genesis* 3: 5); the core of his blessings bears out this innuendo. In Whitman's myth, man is no longer created in God's image but in the Poet's image. Worship of the poet brings about self-liberation, yet this liberation acquires a new tonality, it is understood as liberation away from God, since "I only am he who places over you no master, owner, better, God, beyond what waits intrinsically in yourself" (To You...233).

Emerson defined the poet as "sovereign." He postulated that "the world is nothing, the man is all; in yourself is the law of all nature" (AS 943) and his imperative was to "live after the Infinite law that is in you" (DSA 948). Whitman's "kosmic" poet is the ultimate sovereign. As such he is supreme lawgiver and ruler. The old dispensation allows the concept of imitation, yet not of identification with God. The poet's revolution is complete. He demolishes the last barriers and carries freedom to its ultimate consequences.

The inevitable corollary of the series of "supremes" is in Whitman's formula that "all is eligible to all.... No condition is prohibited, not God's or any" (By Blue 342). Emblematic of Emerson and Whitman's poet-God is his immunity to the ethical law. Characteristic of Emerson's poet is that he is free, "free without any hindrance that does not arise from his own constitution" (AS 943). To him sacredness is "entirely from within" (Self-Reliance 958). In fact, to him, there remains no other law than his own. Similarly, Whitman exalts his absolute freedom: "I have...taken off my hat to nothing known or unknown" (By Blue 351). Moreover, the law within anticipates the Karamazovian "all is lawful."

But what happens when, in the absence of any other authorial voice, the poet embodies the law? Soon, his assertions of exuberant individualism lead to an aggrandizement of the self that opposes his avowed democratic sentiment. Invested with the insignia of absolute power, the poet's pride goes so far as to supersede reality with his will. He readily becomes a Platonic dictator. In Emerson's terms, "his speech is thunder, his thought is law" (Poet 993). Yet this second "law" is the law of the inexorable. The transcendent "transparent eyeball" resumes its stance of a "tyrannous eye" (Poet 997). Whitman prides himself on bringing about a liberation from any decree—"I will make no account of the laws" (Myself and Mine 237)—since no regulation could hamper his absolute freedom, "I help myself to material and immaterial,/No guard can shut me off, no law prevent me" (Song 65). However, once the Poet becomes God, the egalitarian principle is broken. The principle of absolute freedom he has preached so far cannot prevent the poet from his final identification with the law. Whitman's poet "is judgement, (Nature accepts him absolutely,)/he judges not as a judge judges but as the sun falling on a helpless thing" (By Blue 347). Nevertheless, his is not the law of mercy or compassion, but the indomitable, impersonal law of nature, as implacable as fatality itself.

Emerson and Whitman's poet is a great Romantic hero of the order of Prometheus, Don Juan or Faust. They are kindred spirits and belong to the same family of rebels, precursors of the later Nietzschean demiurge and Dostoevsky's demonic nihilists. Emerson and Whitman's poets pertain to the typology of the prodigious son, who breaks free from the larger, general but at the same time external dictates of the father, God and society. Like Faust, the Whitmanian poet is fascinated by utopia and is equally insatiable. In Goethe's *Faust*, Faust's downfall is occasioned the very moment his quenchless spirit can be satisfied. Yet Whitman's poet remains unrivalled; he surpasses by far Faust's inextinguishable thirst for the infinite, and remains unfulfilled, striving for more, even once he has reached the pinnacle of evolution and looks onto its "yawning heights:"

> This day before dawn I ascended a hill and look'd at the crowded heaven,
> And I said to my spirit *When we become the enfolders of those* orbs, and the pleasure and knowledge of every thing in *them, shall we be fill'd and satisfied then?*
> And my spirit said *No, we but level that lift to pass and continue beyond* (Song 84).

Of the three characters—Prometheus, Don Juan and Faust—the hero poet is most akin to Don Juan, in the temptation to do as one pleases and to discard all general considerations external to the self. Both the hero poet and Don Juan refuse to subject themselves to the general dictates of society and religion, and instead forge their own destiny against a universal law. The poet resembles Don Juan, in as far as he champions the principles of the individual, the self against the laws of the impersonal and the universal. Theirs is the defiance of the established order and the mandates of eternal immutable principles at the behest of his Absolute Self. Ultimately, the poet replaces the imperatives of a higher order by man's will to power. Emerson and Whitman are post-Christian. Their affront to the divine is a prelude to the Nietzschean leitmotif, God is dead. More exactly, God has died only to emerge toweringly in the guise of the poet.

In the new mythography, the poet is a rebellious son who will not be punished for his disobedience, but praised. His story is not the story of his fall but of his rise. He is the vanquished Christ who brings victory on earth and the tidings of a Golden Age.

NOTES

1. References to Whitman's works are based on Sculley Bradley's edition of *Leaves of Grass*, hereafter cited parenthetically as LG. The first words of poem titles are indicated parenthetically. Among those most frequently quoted are: "Song of Myself," cited as "Song;" "By Blue Ontario's Shore" as "By Blue" and "Starting from Paumanok" as "Starting."
2. Successive quotations of Emerson's essays refer to Baym's *Norton Anthology*. The titles of Emerson's essays are indicated parenthetically

by the following abbreviations: AS for "The American Scholar," and DSA for "The Divinity School Address."

3. R.W. Emerson. *Essays and Lectures, Representative Men* (New York: The Library of America, 1983) 761.
4. An interesting analysis of Whitman's "evolutionary cosmology" is to be found in Kuebrich 19-26, 53, 105.
5. Lawrence Bueli, "Transcendentalist Catalogue Rhetoric: Vision versus Form" 113-27. Also on the catalogue see John B. Mason, "Walt Whitman's Catalogue: Rhetorical Means for Two Journeys in *Song of Myself*" and Wynn Thomas, *The Lunar Light of Whitman's Poetry* 80.

WORKS CITED

Baym, Nina, *et al.*, eds. *The Norton Anthology of American Literature.* 3rd ed. 2 vols. New York: Norton and Co., 1989.

Bloom, Harold. *Agon: Towards a Theory of Revisionism.* Oxford: Oxford UP, 1982.

Bradley, Sculley and Harold Blodgett, eds. *Leaves of Grass.* New York: Norton and Co., 1973.

Bucke, Richard M. *et al.*, eds. *The Complete Writings of Walt Whitman.* 10 vols. New York: G.P. Putnam's Sons, 1902.

Buell, Lawrence. "Transcendentalist Catalogue Rhetoric: Vision versus Form," *On Whitman: The Best from American Literature.* Ed. Edwin Cady and Louis Budd. Durham: Duke UP, 1987.

Buell, Lawrence. *New England Literary Culture. From Revolution through Renaissance.* Cambridge: Cambridge UP, 1986. 113-27.

Emerson, Ralph. *Essays and Lectures, Representative Men.* New York: The Library of America, 1983.

Fromm, Erich. *You Shall Be as Gods.* New York: Henry Holt & Co, 1991.

Guthrie, W.K.C. *The Greeks and their Gods.* Boston: Beacon Press, 1950.

Kuebrich, David. *Minor Prophecy.* Bloomington: Indiana UP, 1989.

Mailer, Norman. *Armies of the Night.* New York, 1968.

Mason, John B. "Walt Whitman's Catalogue: Rhetorical Means for Two Journeys in *Song of Myself,*" *On Whitman: The Best from American Literature.* Ed. Edwin Cady and Louis Budd. Durham: Duke UP, 1987.

Miller, Hillis. *The Disappearance of God.* Cambridge: Belknap Press, 1963.

Thomas, Wynn. *The Lunar Light of Whitman's Poetry.* Cambridge: Harvard UP, 1987.

7

John Updike's Achievement as a Novelist

S.M.R. AZAM

John Updike started his career as a staff member of a journal called *The New Yorker.* But his sheer brilliance has carried him beyond the confines of journalism. Today he is one of the leading literary figures of America, enjoying a world-wide fame with numerous prizes and awards to his name. During a span of over forty years he has distinguished himself as a writer of profundity, polish and sophistication, displaying tremendous energy and exceptional talent, producing book after book, over forty in number—sixteen novels, several collections of short stories and poems, plays, innumerable critical and prose essays, and children's books. His impressive growth as a writer of high stature, honour and admiration is an obvious testimony to the fulfilment of the great promise he showed when he set out to make his indelible mark in the world:

> The little tyrant's delight in wielding a pencil always carried with it an empathy into the condition of being a pencil; more and more a writer thinks of himself as an instrument, a means whereby a time and place make their mark. To become less and transmit more, to replenish energy with wisdom—some such hope...is the reason why I write (PUP 39).

What makes Updike an immortal writer is his ability to share another person's feelings and emotions as if they were his own. He sees our sadness, our empathy with the pain we are surely suffering in this horrible, crass world. He has real sensitivity, real empathy. Gradually Updike the man grows smaller and smaller and Updike the artist grows bigger and bigger. To replenish energy with wisdom is the crux of his art. No wonder he has grown in critical acclaim and will continue to grow.

However, it must be pointed out that Updike has not always received his commendation. He has been subject to low denunciation as well. But what is remarkable is that he never went out of shape and continued to move from strength to strength. Thus full credit goes to Updike for growing out of the disparaging criticism with equanimity to achieve.

His wide readership includes not only professional critics and students of literature but also a reading public large enough to keep each novel on the best seller list for months. Criticized by some readers for being too melodramatic and by others for being too philosophical, Updike has apparently managed to maintain a delicate balance between the romantic and the reflective, between the appeal of the popular novel and the critical esteem of more esoteric fiction (ASS 389).

The difficulty in understanding Updike's fiction is that the complexity arises out of the suggestive nature of his art. In his case, implication is art. He works with such literary techniques that exploit the devices like dialectical method, irony, parody, fantasy, myth, nostalgia, dreams, allegory, fable and the symbolic motif. The detailed imagery intensifies the impact of the artistic vision in its wholeness. The wealth of minutest details with which he describes scene, setting atmosphere, milieu, characters, and the vast range of his vocabulary do also contribute to the obscurity of his fiction. His unique style, though it has increased the resources of the English language, also creates problems of comprehension as it carries layers of meaning. If one is not clear enough to pick up the tropes of art one is bound to falter and fail. That is why Updike's fiction has been termed esoteric.

Obviously, ambiguity, one of the hallmarks of great art, rules Updike's fiction which raises many vital issues but does not answers them directly. Updike's sharp apprehension of human condition and of reality defies a categorical yes or no, both existing as the two divergent planes of a paradox. Updike quotes Melville to substantiate his firm belief that the puzzle is insoluble, indicating his own middleness between the contrasting points of view: "Yea and Nay—Each hath his way/ But God He Keeps the middle way." Thus, life which is actually a paradox cannot be reduced to a clear-cut division between yes and no, and if any such attempt is made, it would be a great injustice to Updike's rich, wholesome art. What is required is the will to walk simultaneously on the two parallel lines of paradox, maintaining a delicate balance between the two so that one does not fall down on the ground.

It is clear that Updike's achievement of an equilibrium between differing view-points emphasizes his non-committal stance, enabling him to dramatize, in all his novels and short stories, the eccentric particularities of American life in motion. A balanced, unprejudiced, unbiased and open approach to life gives his art flexibility, resilience, durability and the great quality of adjustment. For Updike, life is like a coin with two sides, both being of equal importance and value, and without either of them the coin is not complete but lopsided or incomplete. The fullness of life demands acceptance of juxtapositions and contrasts. Variegation is life of which Updike's fiction is a perfect emblem. Indeed, Updike's account of life is fair and reasonable. He is a disinterested observer.

Moreover, Updike's disinterested view of life makes him totally different from his contemporaries. To Updike, life is not intelligible and transparent but unintelligible and opaque. So the nature of life cannot be grasped by thought, analysis and classification. On the contrary, the secrets of life can only be partially grasped, striking awe and wonder, making every moment significant and exciting with unexpected turns of events, keeping interest and hope alive in the general drama of life. Thus the valiant attempt is to penetrate the deepest secrets of life in order to get to its meaning, significance and worth, not in the manner of scientific analysis and exposition but the way one gazes at Monalisa's famous enigmatic smile which is for all yet for none. The desire to know, to understand, to explore, to learn can be termed as the indomitable spirit of inquisition, the state of contemplation, the tool of knowledge and enlightenment, leading to self-discovery: Who am I? What am I? and Why am I?

As a matter of fact, Updike does not like "the sprouting—off, the conjuring of opinions." He calls this practice of art a "Showbiz" although he is quite aware that this business is not "without a touch of ham." However, in this age of publicity, as a practitioner of art he decries "the drain on the brain, the assumption that a writer is a mass of opinions to be trucked in and carted off for his annual six minutes on the pan—the American talk show." Updike conceives a writer in the following terms:

> He is not; he is a secretor of images, some of which he prays hill have the immortal resonance of Don Quixote's Windmills, of Proust's madeleine, of Huck Finn's raft. As a secretor he must be at heart secret, patient, wicked even. His duty is, in a sense, to turn his back. This is not easy to understand in an era when everybody says "Have a nice day" and even two O'clock in the morning is lit by the phosphorescent glow of money going rotten (10).

Updike's determined intent to remain as "a secretor of images" reminds one of Lord Buddha who maintained a "noble silence" on many of the vital issues with which religion and philosophy have concerned themselves, and when questioned, answered them in paradoxes. Updike, too, is like Buddha in this respect. God, religion, death, dread, guilt, sin, sex, redemption, the light-in-being, immortality, divorce, marriage, morality—Updike has much to say about these age-old cherished topics fundamental to human existence but he deliberately masks them with a veil of silence to evoke richness of meaning in order to attain the immortal resonance of Don Quixote's Windmills, of Proust's madeleine, of Huck Finn's raft. However, the mystery of silence leaves the read, uncertain, gaping and fuming. But Updike comes to the defence of a writer who is a secretor at heart: "it is not the duty of the fiction writer to decide; this stress should not be laid upon him," "the interestingness and the fertility of the puzzle derives from its unsolvability; our pain deserves dramatization only where it is paradoxical" (10).

Thus, Updike's novels have no transparent sides. They justify his definition of a novel where the creator is always hidden behind the mask.

A novel imitates reality in, among other aspects, a certain opacity, a proud opacity. It must come on not wearing its meaning on the sleeve of an introduction but embodying its meaning, or, rather, meaning its existence. Even its imperfections it must wear proudly, as honourable scores. The artist's effort consists not of bringing work to perfection but of bringing it to the point where the creation, not the creator, takes active part in the sentence. The question then becomes not whether I am content but whether the book, or the book case is finished. It is (HSH 857-58).

Updike's novels are like the deep oceans. To find the pearl one must dive into their depths; the survivors are the victors. Thus Updike's novels are meant for exploration. Then their serious and interesting aspects will become obvious. The reader has to think about carefully before he can fully understand them as they contain richness, strength and the great amount of knowledge along with the depths of situation and emotion. What is imperative on the reader is to cover their top and bottom surfaces. That is to say, Updike deals with human life thoroughly and considers all the aspects of it. Besides, opacity may be the high point of imperfection of Updike's novels but they wear it proudly, as an honorable scar, much in the same way as the oceans wear their depth. Updike is not concerned with bringing work to perfection but with the creation of work. The creator is a passive participant in creation. This creation is an imitation of reality. Thus, Updike is concerned with the representation of reality, not in the manner of the Naturalist's but in his own unique, individual way. This is something new in the annals of literary fiction, making Updike interesting and exciting to study and explore. Updike is a realist but of a new order. Updike may be described as a neo-Aristotalean in his fresh approach to the craft of fiction.

The high water mark of Updike is that he does not write "gushers." He writes "books that are hard and curvy, like keys, and that unlock the traffic jam in everybody's head." Something like Emc, only in words, one after the other (874). Updike is clearly in the retrograde business of spinning clouds, syntactic filament by filament, in an age when clouds can be had at the twist of a knob or the push of a button on aerosol can (877). Updike exemplifies Dr. Johnson's famous remarks: "Where there is a difficulty, there is a reward."

The obscurity in Updike's fiction is further complicated by his conception of morality which is not traditional but non-institutional. His protagonists are men of staunch religious faith. But except John Hook, they do not conform to the established social and moral codes. Driven by intense, uncontrollable, obsessive prompting of sex, they are often led to adultery and incest, breaking all limits of moral law and rectitude, not caring for the consequences of their actions that may be detrimental to the moral health of the society they inhabit. What is primary for them is their existence which precedes essence. They can be described as "Christian Existentialists" with firm belief only in God but not in the ordained religions and moral order. Thus Updike's Un-orthodox sense of morality can be best understood in terms of Existentialism as espoused by Kirkegaard and Barth. Harold H. Watts calls Updike "a moralist out of season" (HHW 678-79) and elucidates the complexity involved in comprehending his fiction on account of his unconventional treatment of the conventional view of morality:

> This may not be immediately apparent to some readers who can doubt that there is any link between a continuing moral curiosity and the many passages in the novels which give explicit accounts of sexual success and sexual importance. Yet the sexual adventures of the minister in "A Month of Sundays" are no more exactly set down than are the "spiritual" aspirations that lead the minister to compose discourses that link the presence of sexuality with the advent of Grace. For Updike is not the kind of stoic moralist familiar to us in the eighteenth century and elsewhere who seeks to detect and defend a purely humanistic code of excellence. The code of excellence that reveals itself intermittently in the Updike novels is one

> that has its roots in the "O attitudes" that had their traditional expression in the transports of mystics and in the teaching of the *New Testament.* The minister of *A Month of Sundays* thinks of Barth and Tillich when he is not fornicating and sometimes when he is. Updike provides some of his novels with epigraphs from the *New Testament* and Pascal. And, in the midst of a reported life which seems quite discontinuous with these august phrases, Updike provides flickers of light and inchoate illuminations that direct attention beyond traditional common sense and the current doubt that there is any sense whatever to the lives that a novelist may at present describe (680).

Updike's novels hinge on matter-spirit conflict, and recurrently dramatize this basic dichotomy in their agitated activeness through such protagonists who are torn apart by the polar promptings of body and soul, one pulling the other in the opposite direction. Feeling threatened, alienated, isolated, lonely, angst-ridden, guilt-stricken, the protagonists try to counter the menacing, corrupt world, and in the very process oscillate between faith and sex, between faith and morality, between time and space, between guilt and redemption, between conceivable and inconceivable, between heaven and earth, between this world and the next, between mortality and immortality. Some of the protagonists resolve the tormenting crisis by going for either of the two. George Caldwell chooses divinity in *The Centaur.* But his artist son, Peter, and Rabbit, Joey Piet, Ellellou, Jerry Conant and Henry Bech yield to the natural. The minister Marshfield of *A Month of Sundays* and Roger Lawbert of *Roger's Version* unite the two—the former by sleeping in bed with an imaginary beloved and the latter by committing incest with his step-niece. Only John Hook is free from this conflict.

However, the characters who embrace the physical suggest that the world is doomed and so are its citizens, helplessly caught in the intricate web of disruptive forces unable to consecrate the desecrated world. Though they are the followers of Jesus Christ, yet they do not hesitate to flount his instructions which he gave them in one of his sermons on the mount:

> You did not make the world or determine its nature or the moral laws which govern it. If you are to live in it successfully, you must conform with these laws. If you frame your actions in accordance with them you will be like a man who builds his house on a firm foundation; for you will be living in accordance with the real pattern of the Universe. The stars in their courses will fight for you; you cannot fail. If you do not, you will be like a man who builds on sand, sooner or later, however beautiful and solid it may look, your house will collapse (FCH 102).

Most of Updike's protagonists fail in their spiritual quest and they finally give it up. They go for a world based on socially, morally and religiously unsanctioned sex. They do so because they find the world hollow and purposeless, not catering to their spiritual longings. They build on sand. No wonder their house collapses. This collapse is reflective of the world's collapse. For them the old conventional morality has become worn out and no longer fits the modern man's requirements. This situation is best summed up by the hero of *Marry Me*, Jerry Conant who remarks: "May be our trouble is that we're living in the twilight of an old morality, and there's just enough to torment us, and not enough to hold us in." The world is devoid of substance; the quest for a new order yields to failure and frustration, as the inhabitants of this fast decaying world do not have enough grid in themselves. Significantly, the modern world is characterized by pragmatism. As Updike's characters are impractical, unable to cope with the pragmatism of daily life, they naturally end in failure. In the modern world, success comes from being practical. This is well demonstrated by Rabbit Angstrom who at last becomes rich in *Rabbit is Rich*, the third novel of Rabbit tetralogy.

However, the failure of the quest stresses the more urgent need for a spiritual and moral regeneration. But Updike's protagonists find it immensely difficult to match illusion with reality. This explains why some of the protagonists are failed artists. Joey Robinson, the hero of *Of the Farm* puts it more cogently when he observes that his father would have been a very good craftsman if he had not been given to work with intangibles. So is the case with Joey himself who is a poet manque, and with others—Piet Hanema in *Couples*, Jerry Conant in *Marry Me*. This might as well be extended to Marshfield in *A Month of Sundays* and Ellellou in *The Coup* as they write their own memoirs in exile. The unconducive cultural factors also frustrate their artistic ambitions, best reflected in Henry Bech's writing impasse for thirteen long years. Art is the fixing of a few passing seconds, according to Updike. But his artist protagonists fail to concretize the fleeting time and create shelter for themselves and for others. They burn in the blazing sun and end as tired and exhausted men. The sense of the world's impending doom weights heavily on them but they cannot halt its downward slide or resurrect it. They are left enveloped in gloom and despair, ultimately decaying in death.

However, these characters remind us of Buddhism which is known to be the most mystical of the higher religions, expressed through Lord Buddha's concept of *Nirvana*. The characters' false deaths indicate the achievement of *Nirvana*—the purification of the senses or complete parting with illusions, ushering in a new era of renewal and rebirth. Thus, through the natural, they attain the most profound knowledge, the existential knowledge—the light-in-being. We know that Lord Buddha was perhaps the first existentialist, the attainer of enlightenment for whom the light of life was contained in opposites. For both Lord Buddha and Updike, neither yes nor no but both. Harold H. Watts, too, finds inconclusiveness as the most outstanding feature of Updike's fiction.

Such are most of Updike's novel's: clever narratives that move from narrative to meditation. At first encounter, Updike's work seems to be devoted to the reproduction of textures that are self-evident: textures of the inconclusive, textures composed by the crass indifference of most men to each other. All this is done with brilliance and is right (HHW 680).

However, some of the Updike characters have the Adamic fall, too, suggesting the acquisition of a new kind of awareness, experience and knowledge in spiritual terms. Man sinned in Adam, resulting in guilt, suffering and atonement without which redemption cannot be hoped for. This awareness shows man's limitations before the infinite power and amounts to what is known as self-knowledge. The journey from innocence to experience, from active to passive, from restlessness to rest, from the thick of things to oblivion, indicates the signs of maturity and the advent of Divine Grace.

Nonetheless, Updike's novels, like all other modern novels reflect the chaos that is eating into the very vitals of the modern world. In other words, Updike's novels are testaments to the chaos as described by Richard H. Rupp:

> The complexities of the modern world have increased since 1945. It is a world of confusion—confusion of purpose, uncertain identity, and the wide spread abdication of authority. This confusion extends to the arts and literature in a special way. The contemporary novel seems to offer us unintelligible pictures of an unintelligible world.... Society itself seems formless, fluid, without the comforting assurances of stability and order.... As for feeling, no response to life is prescribed. Sexual perversion, for instance, is a viable option in the novel of our day, at least in reflecting the general pain of loving in a loveless world. To live is to witness the chaos and social relationships in that world; to write is to show that chaos (RHR 17).

Updike's selection of his protagonists as well as his antagonists stresses his underlying conviction of the insurability of the present human condition. Also stressed is the fact that the primal sense of heroism, order, fulfilment and hope has yielded to the powerful impulse of frustration, anarchy and despair. This is expressed in the main characters' realization of their family life as empty, suffocating, burdensome, edging on to clutter and senselessness. Their fascination with immortality, death and the light-in-being is certainly not meaningless but undoubtedly ironical and not coming to any purpose in this insensitive frittering away world. In *Rabbit, Run,* Rabbit's disturbed, painful relationship with his repulsive looking wife, Janice, a symbol of disorder, denying him his hope of a better, unseen world, leads him to Ruth, a whore, with whom he experiences through adultery such sublime love, he had not experienced before that transcends the vestiges of time and gives such ecstasy to his soul that it takes flight and soars towards the unknown. He swings between the calls of society and soul, between Janice and Ruth. When he glimpses the horrible reflection of his wife in his mistress, he runs away from her. He turns his back to the world disappears in oblivion. After a decade Rabbit reappears in *Rabbit Redux* as a passive man having crumbled under the weight of cultural, social and moral disintegration. Now he accepts life as it is. Without any qualms he accepts his sloppy wife when she returns to him after her sojourn with Charlie Stavros. However, Rabbit's sexual fantasies do not fade away. He has sex with his surrogate daughter. He gives shelter to a fiery young Negro with revolutionary ideas. But this revolutionary called the Black Jesus, is shot dead before he could resurrect the broken world. Convinced that the fragmented world cannot be put in order, Rabbit again disappears from the world reappear after a decade in *Rabbit Is Rich*. Now he is rich, satisfied and stable. He continues his spirit of social adjustment. He shows his utmost concern for the future of his son. The chinks of dissatisfaction and disturbance in the family relationships are contemplated by this self-introspective man. But he passes them off from his mind for the sake of relative happiness. This spiritual quester now prefers not to go to church but stay at home. Warming himself by imagining and indulging in sexual exploits as the last resort of sanity in this insane world. After a decade he reappears in *Rabbit at Rest.* He is so overwhelmed with sexual longing that he commits incest with his daughter-in-law. Old, depleted and haggard as he is, he is finally put to rest for ever. Rabbit's gradual decline is symbolic of America's decline. The agitated disordered human life starting with *Rabbit, Run* finds its culmination with Rabbit's death in *Rabbit at Rest.*

Updike's novels, as a whole, envision an entropic or apocalyptic world where Supernaturalism is even a spent force. The grim awareness of disorder all around and of the futility of human existence reduces the sensitive modern man to imbecility, gloom and cynicism. Henry Bech seeks peace in silence and reduction. At the end of *The Poorhouse Fair* the ninety-four year old John Hook finds it useless to impart a word of wisdom to the young director of the poor house, Stephen Conner who professes humanism but denies it to the old inmates about to die: "When would they all die and let the human day dana?" the contemplative Rabbit, growing huge in self-awareness, ultimately comes to realize that his life has at last come to no purpose, like the grass which shines to die. Marshfield and Ellellou find solace in exile. The murder of the Black Jesus puts an end to the last hope of revolution and redemption. The light goes out. The world is left with darkness all around. The only sensible, soothing and passionate thing is despair. According to Harold H. Watts, Updike's fiction expresses a well-bred skepticism as to what is possible for human sensibility in our time (HHW 680). Joyce Carol Oates, while concluding her comments on *The Coup*, asks the question: "Is such cynicism soluble in art?" Her answer is: "Indeed yes."

This means that Updike's refined sensibility, as it filters through his novels, is not that of a writer who has fully acquiesced in the general decay and uncertainty of an era. Rather Updike takes shape as a writer who keeps circling around the modern detritus with a sharp eye for some fragmented persistence of meaning and order (JAC 1378). Thus, Updike's novels reveal his active, sensitive and complex response to, and an earnest desire to come to terms with the grim, almost holocaustic situation that has obtained in the world since World War II. Updike achieves this end through the deft use of myth which, according to T.S. Eliot as he defined it in defence of James Joyce's incomprehensive novel *Ulysses* making use of myth, "is simply a way of controlling, of ordering, of giving a shape and a significance to the immense panorama of futility and anarchy which is contemporary history." "It is at this level that Updike's intuition of structural possibilities have settled," according to Jackson I. Cope who defines "structural possibilities" as patterns and parallels and a hint of generation they generate (1378).

Updike's very first novel *The Poorhouse Fair* signals the arrival of a major writer who is daring, innovative, experimental, imaginative and mature at the very young age of twenty eight. Modelled on the cool surface of some contemporary French novels, it is an anti-novel, anti-utopian in nature approximating the French novelist Nalhalie Sarrute's description of the modern novelistic predicament. It sets the zone, tenor, texture and colour of the ensuing Updike novels. What it envisages characterizes all the novels: The world is moving fast towards its thermal death, and the forces of entropy cannot be thwarted. The fierce clash between religion and science occupies the centre stage of Updike's fiction. This is done brilliantly by setting two sets of opposing characters in motion, one negating the other generating tension which makes the novels vibrating and pulsating. The protagonists are men of belief whereas the antagonists are men of disbelief. According to Joyce B. Markle, in Updike's fiction:

> Also chronicled is his reluctant emergence from the Christianity which seemed so natural to previous Americans, into the practical but comfortless existentialism which marks the scientific modern era. This dialectic—between the reassuring God-given order of religion and the man-made order of the sciences—forms the basic tension of Updike's fiction (JBM 390).

In Updike's fiction, religion is the reassurance of a meaningful, substantial existence, as John Hook affirms in *The Poorhouse Fair* "There is no goodness without belief." The very talent of Rabbit Angstrom is that he gives people hope. He castigates Jack Eccles for failing in his duty as a clergy man to burn people with faith. In *Roger's Version* Roger Lambert outrightly rejects the young physicist, Dale Kohler's assertion that he can prove the existence of God through scientific experiments because no power on earth can make him visible if he has decided to remain invisible. Rogar calls Kohler a heretic. Therefore, "religion gives hope and a sense of reward beyond the immediate; it is an intrinsic excellence of an ultimate standard."

In religion, the calm forbearance of pain is a necessary spiritual condition for immortality of soul. To Updike's heroes, adversity has its uses; more than it crushes. Obviously, in the religious world, suffering or pain is the most valuable and sacred human possession. Piet Hanema, the Calvinistic hero of

Couples believes that suffering in any form is good for character as it gives solidity and solace. The hero of *The Coup*, a devout Muslim, regards suffering as the founding unit of life and faith and looks to the poor and the deprived with respect as they are the torch-bearers of heaven. The hero of *Bech: A Book* and *Bech is Back*, Henry Bech, a famous Jewish American novelist, sees happiness as the enemy of truth. Joey Robinson, the hero of *Of the Farm* values pain most as he deliberately cuts his cheeks while shaving his beard. So is true of George Caldwell in *The Centaur* of Tom Marshfield in *A Month of Sundays*, Harry Rabbit Angstrom in all the four Rabbit novels. The paramount significance of suffering as the cementing force of life is well-presented by John Hook, the hero of *The Poorhouse Fair*: Pain has held the generation together. In Updike's fiction, Suffering is the food of religion. According to the famous Urdu poet, Mirza Ghalib, "The pleasure for a drop of water is to disappear in the ocean, the expansion of pain beyond its limit is the medicine. Indeed, in the realms of mystics and saints, pain is pleasure. The continual self-sacrifice, turning oneself to ashes before the Almighty."

On the other hand, in Updike's fiction, science negates what religion affirms. Thus, religion is of no use to science which, according to Joyce B. Markle, "thrives in a cynical era, where it can demonstrate the workability of its propositions, and fits man nonchalantly into the physical universe of matter and motion, chemicals and processes, but it is cold and sterile, denies both hope and anguish, and gives man no reassuring way to deal with the fact of his own mortality" (390). In the world of science, pain is an evil, and the very elimination of pain means the elimination of evil. Stephen Conner relieves the diseased cat of its lingering pain by putting to death. He intends to do the same with the old dying inmates of the poor house who resemble the diseased cat. Conner gives hatred instead of love, torture instead of sympathy, death instead of life. He burns the *Bible* to warm himself in the cold. He abhores the religious tenet that dropping a kind word is better than a thousand deeds. "No pain and above all no waste" is the new scientific creed held by Conner and shared by all other antagonists. Freddy in *Couples* finds a new religion of pleasure based on free sex where couples exchange their wives and husbands without any compunction. It is a world of sodom and gonorrhea: the new Bible is the erotic magazine. Jack Eccles in *Rabbit, Run,* Zimmerman in *The Centaur,* Ned Bork in *A Month of Sundays,* Richard in *Marry Me,* Michael Ezna in *The Coup,* Dale Kohler in *Roger's Version*—all of them display the secular anti-humanistic attitude of Stephen Conner. All the antagonists to whom the ultimate intrinsic standard is pleasure not pain are guided by a atheistic humanism, cruel in nature.

It must be pointed out that Updike delivers no directive, or homily, or sermon, or message to the world. This attitude perhaps springs from the conviction that the world which is crazy and goofy can only be experienced. That is why Updike strikes a draw between the opposites. The reader is left to choose his own course of thesis, or of anti-thesis, or of both, that is, synthesis.

Actually, Updike works in the mould of the French novelist Proust whose profound influence can be felt in Updike's mixture of nature lyricism and wry psychology. Updike's artistic instrument, like that of Proust, is telescopic, directed upon time. The protagonists of both the novelists are in quest of Time Lost as they frequently turn to the past to regain it. In nostalgia, they find peace from the horrible present. Many of Updike's protagonists regain time through their false deaths and return to work with fresh vision, for example, George Caldwell in *The Centaur*. Art, to both Updike and Proust, is the conquest of the tyrannical Time, the fixing of a few passing seconds or the solidification of illusion into reality. As for Updike, fiction is an equivalent of reality; he, like Proust, places "beneath the melody of a plot a counter melody of imagery, interlocking images which rise to the top and become the plot." Finally, this confusion is treated as the theme itself, "by showing a population of characters whose action were all determined at the deepest level, by nostalgia, by a desire to get back to dive, each into the springs of their private imagery."

However, Updike differs from Proust in his achievement as a novelist. That is, Updike achieves in his fiction what his alter ego, Henry Bech, intended to do: the creation of a hum, a hum perhaps spiritual twin to the rumble of the IRT under Broadway.... The hum, the background radiation to the universe he was trying to create, was, if not the meaning of life, the tenor of meaninglessness in our late-twentieth century, post-numinous, industrial-consumeristic civilization, North American branch, Middle Atlantic Subdivision (BIB 10). This is best exemplified by the quintessential Updike hero, Harry Rabbit Angstrom. Like Rabbit, America is rich but hollow inside, morally and spiritually bereft at heart; the achieved stability is just a mask.

However, in his overt Virtuosity, Updike seems to declare a formal allegiance to James Joyce, the central figure of the modernistic tradition in fiction. The schematic subdivisions of Time in Updike's novels reflect the Joycean influence. The use of myth and the resultant incomprehensiveness link Updike with Joyce. Interestingly, both the writers have outraged critical opinion on account of obscurity in their fiction. Nonetheless, both Updike and Joyce have been accepted as major novelists of great impact. Yet, there is a marked difference between Joyce and Updike: Joyce attempts a synthesis of all existence; Updike leaves the contraries as they are. However, Updike is also a Joyce in his fertile inventiveness. This fact is borne by all his novels. For example, the use of the present tense in the Rabbit novels (they are written in the historic present). In *Rabbit, Run* it is primarily used "to emphasize how the zigzagging hero lived in the present." Updike points to the vital significance of the present tense by quoting Joyce Cary who was the first to use it in his remarkable novel, *Mr. Johnson*:

> It can give to the reader that sudden feeling of insecurity (as if the very ground were made only a deeper kind of darkness) which comes to a traveller who is bushed in an unmapped country, when he feels at once that not only has he utterly lost his way, but also his own identity.

The feelings expressed in Cary's passage is embodied by Rabbit Angstrom whose continual running is a vehement protest against a spiritual and moral wasteland which dries man's urge for fertility, order, a clean way of life, resulting in loss of path and identity, making him a Dalai Lama who is an alien in his own land and insecure in other lands. The story of the traveller, Rabbit Angstrom, "bushed in an unmapped country," is the story of every modern man. In fact, Rabbit is a quintessential everyman or Everyman incarnate.

Nevertheless, numerous examples of Updike's daring, innovative and technical powers can be cited from his books. Some of these are: the overt and oblique use of the classical and Christian myths in various novels; the use of obituary and the present tease in two separate chapters in *The Centaur* and in the same novel the use of surrealistic, cubistic, and double-focus techniques; the shape of *Of the Farm* as "X;" the two Appendices at the end of *Bech: A Book*; the use of the narrative techniques of four different points of view relating to four characters in *Marry Me* indicating four different doctrinal positions and achieving one with the other various ecunemical combinations, and in the same novels the three different endings, and the five chapters symmetrically alternative acquiring the proportion of a diadem in their lengths; the effective use of fantasy, the creation of Ellellou as a mad man and the mixture of Islam and Marxism in *The Coup*; the use of footnote and allusion in many novels; epigraphs affixed to every novel. What is most significant is that these things are not there in the novels as decorations, embellishments, or mere literary displays of virtuosity but they form the integral part of the smooth carpented design.

In fact, Updike used his immense technical prowess to provide the concrete rendering of the fragmented human experience—to put "a heap of broken images" artistically in order. That is to say, Updike's outstanding experimental ability leads a certain precocious power to his evocative art which goes beneath the surface of things, not a layer or two, but very deep where he is able to locate his own unique vision of reality. The reader just marvels at the revealed reality when he goes inside. However, Updike's lavish, elaborate metaphorical Proustian style, his Joycean and Calvinistic imagination, his Joycean treatment of sex, his Henry Greenian factual accuracy and precocity, his deep Hawthornian concern with religion, his

Falubertian depiction of hidden man, his Kafkan awareness of modern man's anguish and isolation, his Pascalian grasp of paradoxical human condition, his Kierkegaardian understanding of 'Angst,' guilt and the definition of goodness, his Barthian concept of God and morality, his Nabokovian approach to novel as Chess puzzles, his Shakespearean art of characterization, his Homeric view of the Narrator's presence in the work of art, his Platonian concept of the cave man, his protagonist; Aristotelian outlook of life, and his own vividly created unforgettable characters—these are some of the vistas which awaken the reader to the enduring qualities of Updike's works; they have a genius, they will pass into the realm of immortality.

WORKS CITED

B. Markle, Joyce. On John Updike in *The American Short Story*, Vol. I. Ed. Calvin Skaggs: New York: Dell Publishing Co. 1977.

H. Watts, Harold. On John Updike in *20th Century Fiction*. Ed. James Vinson. The Macmillan Press Ltd. 1983. London and Basing Stoke.

Happold, F.C. *Mysticism*. Harmondsworth: Penguin Books Ltd. 1981.

H. Rupp, Richard. *Celebration in Post-War American Fiction 1945-67*. Coral Gables, Florida: University of Miami Press, 1970.

H. Watts, Harold. *20th Century Fiction*, 680.

I. Cope, Jackson. On John Updike in *The Contemporary Novels*. Ed. James Venson. St. James Press: London, 1976.

Updike, John. *Bech is Back*: New York: Fawcett Crest, 1982.

——. *Picked up Pieces*, New York, Knopf, 1975.

——. *Hugging the Shore*: Harmondsworth Penguin Books Ltd. 1985.

8

JOHN A. WILLIAMS: THE NOVELIST

JYOTI MISHRA

John A. Williams is an outstanding American author, one of the major black novelists of the contemporary American literary scene. He is an accomplished writer like Richard Wright, Ralph Ellison, James Baldwin and Ishmael Reed and commands an interracial as well as international audience. Author of eleven novels and other works, editor of several reputed literary magazines, distinguished Professor of English, La Guardia College, City University of New York (1973-75): visiting Professor of University of Hawai, Honolulu (Summer 1974) and recipient of National Institute of Arts and Letters Grant (162) and Syracuse University Outstanding Achievement Award (1970), Williams is remarkable for mirroring the changing focus of black anger. As a novelist he writes in the realistic mode and is regarded as a master of characterization. He views art as political serving political ends more graciously than those of the muses.

He is concerned with social and political themes in his fiction. However, philosophical and psychological issues do also give meaning to these themes. The situation of the blacks-supplied Williams with a perfect metaphor for studying the nature and influence of history and for testing whether man either as an individual or as a race can transcend the nightmarish role that history seems to have determined for him. All Williams's characters, to one degree or another try to break free from the limitations that history and race have placed upon them. Williams is always aware of the social insufficiencies which are a result of political manipulation. Therefore, his socio-political vision relates to a larger humanistic vision. In *One for New York* published as *The Angry Ones* (the title given by the publisher for making it a bestseller) Steve Hill, the protagonist insists upon and claims the socio-political and economic rights that have been denied the blacks in American. His triumph is that he marries the woman of his choice and finds a good job. In other words, Steve Hill is "not thinking about a revolution; he is thinking about three squares and a nine-to-five routine." Ultimately he gets what he thinks is necessary to be a human being.

Steve Hill is an enthusiastic and enterprising young negro who enters the publishing business in New York and discovers that there is little opportunity for a black. He has to toil hard to get a job suffering a series of denials and modifications. He is taken to be a messenger and asked to leave the packet on the table. This is because negroes are usually serving as messengers; being a black, Steve is bound to be a messenger. Because of discrimination which is a result of political manipulation, Steve Hill takes a job with a vanity publishing company, Rocket.

The status of *Night Song* (1961) his second novel is dubious at best. It almost won Williams the Prix de Rome from the American Academy of Arts and Letters and received favourable reviews but later critics dismissed it as an "apprentice work," derivative, literary and ineptly political. Whatever be the merits or demerits, *Night Song* deals with the jazz experience, a crucial aspect of black culture but also reflecting certain aesthetic problems of technique black novelists have to face around 1960. This was a year which signified a crucial juncture between social criticism, Bohemianism and Civil Rights Movement. The so-called "protest novel" a majority term for minority fiction and itself an example of cultural hegemony, seemed to have reached its end not so much because the causes of its emergence had disappeared, but because the cold war climate of the fifties had made black social criticism and leftist attitudes in the vein of Richard Wright or the early Chester Himes something "un-American" and had brought more acceptable writers like Ralph Ellison and James Baldwin who were willing to disclaim the protest tradition to the foreground. Williams states the underlying conditions very clearly:

"They, Baldwin and Wright, were a generation apart, but they remained victims. They were artists, writers, yet they knew that only one of them at a time, were it James Baldwin, Langston Hughes, Chester Himes, Ralph Ellison, or Richards Wright, could be, would be allowed to be, the black writer of the moment. America was not geared nor did it wish to be geared for the spectacle of more than one black writer at a time...."

This process had displaced the naturalistic conventions, channelising black grievances into more acceptable literary conventions. On the other hand, there was the new Beat Movement and the new East Village Bohemia catering around St. Mark's place in places like the Five Spot Cafe, the Cedar Tavern, the Eighth Street bookshop or Micky Ruskin's Tenth Street coffee house. Here such diverse writers as Norman Mailer, Jack Kerouac, Allen Ginsburg, LeRoi Jones, Calvin Hernton and David Henderson lived, worked and met each other. Black writers founded the society of Umbra and published little magazines like *Yugen* or *The Floating Bear*. Williams makes this new bohemia around St. Mark's place the theme and setting of *Night Song*. He takes one of the cultural heroes of the beat movement as the novel's secret hero, that is, Charles Christopher Parker, Jr. Popularly called as Charlie Parker or Yardbird or Bird. In the novel he is Richie Stokes, the Eagle.

However, *Night Song* is neither a beat or jazz novel, nor a protest novel, nor the novel of an angry young man, though it shows traits of all these conventions. Unlike Dorothy Barker's *Young Man with a Horn* (1938) which sets some of the conventions for the Jazz novel, *Night Song* does not make a thinly disguised jazz musician the central character of the book. In fact, critics have seen different characters as the hero of the novel. For Ronald Walcott *Night Song* is basically a novel of Keel Robinson's identity quest between black and white of his generation after having been emasculated by a white racist society. Earl A. Cash sees *Night Song* primarily as a mythic initiation of a prejudiced white David Hillary into a new knowledge of self. For Jerry J. Bryant, the novel has two main characters—both black and both suffering heroically—the jazz musician Richie Stokes and Keel Robinson. David Hillary serves as a white foil. The contradictions between these interpretations are resolved when *Nigh Song* is viewed using the Jamesian convention of telling the story of a group of closely interrelated people in multi-perspective or different point of views. Another title for *Night Song* might well have been "The Wings of the Eagle," according to Wolfgang Karrer.

The problem *Night Song* poses is what happens when two whites and two blacks meet in a situation, the night world of Bohemia where the "normal"—relations of racist domination are momentarily inverted, a black man loves and marries a white woman and a white man works as a waiter for a black proprietor? Both sexual domination and domestic service have long characterized relations between blacks and whites in United States. The solution *Night Song* offers is this: love whether as interracial sex or help and solidarity between black and white can be stronger than racism as in the case of Della Madison and Keel Robinson. However, this solution appears partially effective because Richie Stokes, the Eagle still faces the institutional racism. Even if the disc jockey Rod Tolen, the jazz critic Stanley Crane or the recording agent Moe Alvin could be made to act in solidarity with Eagle instead of exploiting him, the institutional framework of racism in education, employment and justice would not disappear quickly.

John A. Williams once complained that White critics tend to compare Black writers only with other Black writers, thus cementing segregation and double standards in criticism as in life. *Night Song* provides an excellent opportunity not only in technique or discourse but also in subject matter or story for a comparison with other fictional accounts of Charlie Parker who remains the most important influence in modern jazz and one of the greatest musicians that United States has ever produced. Although there are a few stories about Charlie Parker—*Sparrow's Last Jump* by Elliot Grennard, Jack Kerouac's *On the Road*, John Cellon Homes's *The Horn*, etc. *Night Song* remains the only black contribution.to Charlie Parker fiction.

Night Song seems to reflect where John A. Williams—and with him Baldwin, Smith and other black writers—stood in the early sixties. It is also an example of the limitations audience and publishers imposed on a black writer without any bargaining power.

At a time when many black writers seem torn between political commitment and literary calling, John A. Williams' seems able to follow both. His growing commitment to social and political issues has not apparently affected his productivity as a novelist. Social issues in his fiction become significant literary themes as well. Like Baldwin and Barakka, Williams must be seen and honoured as a hero to apprentice writers desperately searching for strong models of black manhood. For it is not easy to be black and a man and a writer in a culture that emasculates of colour so many restrictions. In Williams' work there is a strength united with intelligence, literary skill with scholarship aimed at restoring black self-esteem. His work has permanence endowed with form and expression. This is best expressed by his monumental novel *The Man Who Cried I Am.*

9

The Image of City in the Novels of James Baldwin

A.K. PANDEY

City, a human artifact, which has become an object in the world of nature, has been man's visible architect. The most basic of these cities is the interpretation of the past and the present. On the one hand there is visible cities of street and buildings. On the other hand there are the subconscious currents arising in the minds of the city's living inhabitants from this combination of past and present. These currents include the cities with the realm of the dead through its temple cemetery and ceremonies as well as its old buildings and its function as the seat of secular power, embodied in monarchs, governments and banks and other social and economic institutions.

The city is, as Joseph Rykwert characterizes it a curios artifact "compounded of willed and random elements in perfectly controlled" (AC 346). It has been called a 'state of mind' (Robert 1). The image of city has got a lot of reflection of the mood and temperament of the author and his society. A host of American cities, despite all differences in size, location, or composition, continually try to validate the claims that they are typical authentic American communities. They balance what they are and what they feel stand for against a tacitly accepted formula of American values and national purposes.

Through intellectual history the city as an idea has been haunted by double moral judgment. American's too these ambiguities scriptures, as Maynard Mack says "begin with a garden and ends with a city" (Mack 3). This ambiguity of American urbanity and American values is significantly reflected in a lively contention over which city best deserves the title "most American." The admirers of Chicago, New York, Kansas, and Detroit, at least, claim honors for the city of their choice. Chicago once called "the City of Gardens"—still boasts that it is the city of the Praise and lays claims to a characteristic friendliness and infirmity that make it off from, New York or Boston. New York is partly or wholly not American, or even un-American. The grounds of attack and defense bring to sharp focus the ambiguity and clash of American values.

James Baldwin the spokesperson of the Black has presented the image of city to reflect the two worlds that he saw and tried to get a solution to the problem of race. James Baldwin's first novel, *Go Tell It On The Mountain* is based on the real city of New York especially Harlem. Baldwin has based his novel's meaning on one of the richest, the most complex of configuration in the history of the thought, the idea of the city, People, assert that New York represents the nation at its most civilized and most creative; that it dominates the nation in every way; and that more different kinds of Americans, drawn from regions, live New York than in any other metropolis.

The setting of the novel is the real city of New York especially Harlem brings out the estate of the mind and the history as well. The real cities have had their own individual history. They have been plagued and bound, moved and refounded, expanded and contracted and being subjected to all the vicissitude of real objects in the world. On the other hand, the association and resonance of the city as an image, especially in literature seem to reflect attitude, which appear to have changed the little scenes beginning the western culture. New York, the real city in the novel, Go Tell It On The Mountain brings history and ideas of Harlem. The tension in Go Tell It On The Mountain arises from the clash between conception of the earthly city: New York versus Harlem and New York versus itself. New York is a city, which has been passionately and repeatedly denied essential American status while its admirers have proclaimed it the greatest city in America.

Baldwin juxtaposes two cities, the earthly and heavenly and together, they help to focus the novel's various things: father and son, individual and community, the sacred and profane. Baldwin obviously depends upon Saint Augustine's two cities to give structure to the themes. Augustine tells the whole truth about the earthly city. At the end of Go Tell It On The Mountain, John Grime, the young protagonist will have a transcendent experience reminiscent of John of Patmos's vision in the book of Revelation. Nevertheless his moment of truth will be fought with ambiguity, for the new Jerusalem, which he sees as its psychological roots in the very earthly city, which he rejected.

The Negro spiritual Go Tell It On The Mountain, whose title Baldwin appropriated for his novel, presents an Augustine view of man's lot in the world. For August, the true Christian in only a pilgrim in this life but a citizen in the next (Saint Ch. 1). A wayfarer and a 'seeker,' he would be lost without Christ's help, but Christ has graciously shown him 'the way.' Thus, he is capable of achieving a heavenly city within himself, yet it is in constant peril form the evil forces outside 'the city wall.'

The city wall in the novel also refers to the Negro Church the community of true believes who do daily battle with the frightening reality of Harlem. "The Temple of the Fire Baptist" stands on a comer "Facing the hospital to which criminal wounded and dying were carried almost every night." The hospital is an apt symbol, for Harlem is the earthly city sickened unto death.

John Grimes is also in the struggle of himself, with his stepfather and his home—New York, the earthly city. He wants to embrace the earthly city to escape Gabriel's circumscribed world. He cannot free himself from seeing this city through Gabriel's eyes. His response to the world in the given circumstances show his inability to accept either view of the earthly city: a place of liberation or a place of damnation (Strauss 5).

"City can be interpreted in its past and present, history. On the one hand there is visible city of streets and buildings, frozen forms of energy, fixed at different times in the past and around which the busy kinetic energy of the present swords. On the other hand, there are the subconscious currents, arising in the minds of the cities, living inhabitants from this combination of past and present. In the scene, which takes place in the central park, on his birthday, the Saturday afternoon, John climbs his favorite hill, which overlooks New York (the enemy which he hates), running to the top, he is overcome by feelings of wonder and power as he gazes upon the sublime vista of the city. Suddenly, he has an urge "to throw himself head long in to the city that glowed before him." This, he thinks, is the "shining city, which his ancestors had seen with longing from far away." Now "it is his: the inhabitants of the city told him, it was his; he had but to run down, crying and they would take him to their heart and show him wonders—his eyes had never seen" (GTOM 33).

The glories of paradises were 'unimaginable,' John concludes, but 'the city was real.' Ironically, John cannot imagine a celestial city because in his mind Christianity cannot be separated from the hellishness of his father's house. Thus he has been given a past, ancient history of the city (the real city), which he finds suitable.

Through the image of New York City, it's Harlem scenario, temples, 42nd street, 5th avenue, library; Baldwin tries to symbolize the clash in the mind of John, the protagonist, the nigger. "Niggers did not live on these streets," John thinks; now sounding like Gabriel. "Nor were they allowed to enter the wonderful shops and apartments: 'Not today' and he fears his stepfather's laughter, No, nor tomorrow neither."

Baldwin describes the Harlem Scenario in his essay "Fifth Avenue, Uptown" which he grew:

> The avenue is elsewhere, the renowned and elegant Fifth. The area I am describing, which in today's gang parlance, would be called "the turf" is bounded by Lenox Avenue on the west, the Harlem river on the east, 135th street on the north, and 130th street on the south. We never lived beyond these boundaries; this is where we grew up. Walking along 145th Street, for example, familiar as it is, and similar, does not have the same impact because I do not know any of the people on the block.... All along the street there are

> people who watch me grow up, people who grew up with me, people I watched grow along with my brothers and sisters; and sometimes in my arms...their children, a riot, a forest of children who include my niece and nephews (FAU 206).

Underlying the cosmogony of the founding of the ancient city is the idea that the city necessity represents a separation from the world of nature, the imposition of man's will, on a natural order, created by a divinity. The founding as an act of interference in the divine order also involves a sense of guilt. This guilt might be founded by murders. In Genesis, the city founder is Cain, Romulus was also a fratricide founder, and Theusius a patricide founder. In the care of Baldwin he tries to find a city of his forefathers and his conflict with his stepfather.

Baldwin's second novel *Giovanni's Room* which takes place outside America, a city in France, shows his longing for the people of his country but it was also a transaction of author's mind to have a relations with the white. It is the first novel of its kind with homosexuality its prime concern. Baldwin's other novels like *Tell Me How Long The Train's Been Gone* and *Another Country* are presented under the background of the city of New York. In *Tell Me How Long The Train's Been Gone* Barbara comes from Kentucky. This novel is related Baldwin's vision on art and artist.

Leo, the protagonist, presents the prison hall as the 'City College:'

> "Alas he was there; the building turned out to be City College; my brother was on a prison farm in the Deep South, working in the fields" (Train's 8).

Baldwin's agony can be seen in the following lines in the novel *Tell Me How Long The Train's Been Gone*:

> "I really can't bear any of the American cities I know, and I know, or at least I've been traveled through most of them. And most of them seem very harsh and hostile, and they are exceedingly ugly. When an American city has any character, any flavor at all. It's apt to be in the case, for example, of Chicago, rather like a soup has everything in it

> but which is now old, tepid and rancid, which all the ingredients turned sour. All of the American cities seem boiling in a kind of blood pudding, thick, sticky, foul and pungent, and it can make you very sad to walk through, say, New Orleans and ask yourself just why a city with no unconquerable physical handicaps, after all, should yet be so uninhabitable. Some key, I suppose is afforded by the faces, which also seem uninhabitable—at least by any of the more promising human attitudes" (TMLT 272).

The 'City of refuse' in the Christian sense is contrasted in this final section of the novel with the city of refuge represented by the new, youthful Militants of Black Christoph—(a name suggesting 'Black Christ'). This change can be seen as the evolution of Baldwin and his ideas.

In "Tell Me How Long The Train's Been Gone," Baldwin says:

> "I am beginning to believe that a landscape is not a reflection of the sensibility of the people who live in it—certainly this is what one is watching as one crosses their forests and plains, vineyard and mountains, cities, tunnels, towns" (TMLT 142).

Baldwin also discusses the landscapes of other countries to show their moods. Like "French landscape...larger vision...in the way French poodles operate as accessories to the wardrobes of their owners." Swiss landscape is ordered, nothing could be more remote from passion-people who cannot make love make money—any it is designed to advertise one of the most flagrantly fraudulent Eden's in our unhappy history. The Italian landscape is ragged, wild, unpredictable, like the landscape of Spain, the landscape of Africa...." He further shows his American dream, "A day may come, but not for me, when the American South will be habitable" (TMLT 142-143).

Since the novel presents the life of Italians and other Europeans it is very quite obvious Baldwin is referring to his background of influences that he had from Europe.

The image of city occurs in the novels of Baldwin to refer to the past history of the Black people. But he never recognizes himself with the identity of Africa. It is the American nationality that he has always in mind. It is in France that comes to know his real identity and hates to be so. Cities like Kentucky, New York and frequent references to the South America reflect his mind and his past, from where he cannot tear himself.

If Beale Street Could Talk takes place in the city of Attica. The famous Beale Street is in Memphis. W.C. Handy wrote about the street:

> *If Beale Street Could Talk*
> Married men have to take their beds and walk.

Baldwin takes the problem of understanding both white and black to the streets. The novel has nine chapters, each showing nine months of the baby in womb. *If Beale Street Could Talk* presents the real city and its impact with a feminist approach to the city and its suffering.

Baldwin points out to the real problem of America which has proved itself as a place of inequality and opportunities of the limited. He says:

> "It is a terrible, an inexorable, law that one cannot deny the humanity of another without diminishing one's own: in the face of one's victim, one sees oneself. Without through the street of Harlem and see what we, this nation, have become" (Price 213).

The prime concern of Baldwin is to find a city for both the black and white, which is reflected in his novels also. The most popular novel *Another Country* is also in the background of the real city of New York. It is another aspect of the novel in which he tries to find a solution to the problem of race. New York is the greatest and richest city. But this city itself might be described as a mere chessboard, of straight canyons imprisoned within gigantic walls, throbbing with a life, dynamic, stirring eyes—but beautiful. Baldwin wants to make this beautiful the image of the real city for both, the black and the white.

In his last novel *Just Above My Head* Baldwin points out to tweive gates to the city. This image of the city is marked with the vision of Baldwin who wanted a city for next generation:

> My heart thundered, and the church, I silence, thundered. One day we are going to wake up in this strong city and see the lord's deliverance! Our children won't be hungry no more.... Blessed be the Lord! For His marvelous kindness, in this strong city. The strong city... (JAMH 109).

He wants this city to be tumbling for the new generation:

> I believe, I can hear...marching around the walls of a strong city, blowing his trumpet outside the wall of a strong city, and I hear somebody telling me how the walls of that city come tumbling down. That strong city (69).

Baldwin discusses the *street* in his essay "No name in the street." He says, "No Name in the Street" is a personal book, my own testimony to show the holocaust (*Stud Tarkel 1961*). But in the novels Baldwin wants to go (Go Tell It On The Mountain), to tell (Tell Me How long the Train's Been Gone), to talk (If Beale Street Could Talk) in the streets for a new America for the next generation in a *real, strong city* for the another generation (Another Country) just above his head (Just Above My Head), with a subconscious currents arising in the minds because people within different social structure will inevitably differ in their perception of city; in what they can and cannot see, in what they wish to preserve as collective memory and what they wish to forget.

WORKS CITED

Anatomy of Criticism. Princeton Univ. Press.

Baldwin, James. *Tell Me How Long The Train's Been Gone.* New York: Dial Press, 1968.

——. *Go Tell It On The Mountain.* New Yorrk : Dial Press.

——. *Just Above My Head.* New York: Dial Press, 1978.

"Fifth Avenue, Uptown." *In The Price of The Ticket.*

Maynard, Mack. "The garden in the City: Retirement and politics in the later poetry of Pope." Toronto Univ. Press, 1969.

Robert, Park. *et al. The City Chicago.* University of Chicago Press, 1967.

Saint, Augustine. De Christie Dei, Book 15, Chapter 1.

Strauss, A.L. *Images of the American.*

10

KATHERINE ANNE PORTER: ART OF CHARACTERIZATION

ASTHA SUMAN

As a fiction writer Porter is superb. Earliest Porter has presented herself as a stylist but later on she has established herself as a scholar. There are two long collections of short stories in which her characters slightly differ on the surface level but going deep in them, they are ultimately the same. In her fiction what is most significant is the tension between the vision of love and the actual experience of love. The characters try to realize the ideal possibilities of love. In her early work this pursuit is vigorous and intense. But gradually the disparity between the imagined and the actual increases to the point of frustration. It points not only to the fate of a single person, but to a larger social failure. Porter's view of life is realistic and an optimistic. She writers on the real surface of life and never flies high in the imaginary world.

Katherine Anne Porter is basically a story-teller. What is so specific about her stories is that it is not at all burdened with unnecessary characters rather it introduces only that much of characters which the story demands. There is always a hidden message in her stories. That she is a hard realist is well reflected in her stories. Our society has become polluted and it is still going in the negative direction but the hard fact is that we do not have any option save adjusting with it either willingly or unwillingly. We are basically social beings. So, Katherine Anne Porter shows the necessity of adjustment though sometimes with the wrong things for maintaining our peace and existence in this changing society. She always draws her themes and characters from the real world.

In her stories Katherine Anne Porter always presents the family supported in its evil work by other institutions—social, political and religious. Her treatment of evil is just as her treatment of corruption in politics and religion. She always holds an implicit vision of deal that has been vitiated, betrayed, or perverted. She often deals with an almost obsessive preoccupation with family life, and with the struggle of the individual to maintain a personal identity—either within the family, or if need be, in anguished rebellion against it. In almost all of her stories, early or late, this theme appears more or less prominently. The consistency of her concern with it overrides all ethnic, regional, religious, and economic distinctions. Mexican, Texans; White and black; German and Irish immigrants; farmers in Texans and Connecticut; Southern and Middlewestern school teachers and artists and journalists living in Mexico, Denver, New York, and Berlin, Protestants and Catholics and atheists—all, for good and ill, carry with them throughout their lives the burden of family consciousness.

As Katherine Anne Porter represents in her fiction, the lot of men who are generally unhappy; her character's moments of joy are extremely rare—although it ought to be added that the joy is totally convincing when does it occur and the more to be appreciated for the very fact of its rarity. And, if the family itself is not the root of quite all the human wrongs she writers about, still it is seldom that anyone in her stories is helped by his family to cope with the evils that have their source elsewhere in nature and society. The family situation, either present or remembered, is at least a secondary source of the protagonist's unhappiness in almost all of the stories. In almost half of them, the hideous institution is the very fountainhead of misery. The theme in Porter's fiction are illustrated by her characters.

Katherine Anne Porter is a symbolic writer as the titles of her stories suggest. Porter's first short stories collection published as "Flowering Judas" well shows the depth of the meaning. Flower is somewhat a positive term whereas Juda as betrayer always comes in the negative sense. The title immediately suggests the arch betrayer of all time—Judas Iscariot. The Judas tree is the red bud tree from which Christ's betrayer, Judas hanged himself. It is an example of Miss Porter's use of traditional symbols in mythic stories. The theme in Miss Porter's story, is an obvious reference to the Gospel, as this theme studies the mind of a breading traitor to a theoretically idealistic cause. A word of caution—Porter never imposed a symbol on a story but used the symbolic interpretations of actual objects. The symbolic pattern emerged as the story was written. In fact, the title Flowering Judas was given to the story after it was completed. It shows that the betrayal is the thing that is going and flourishing in this present world. Such a flower of betrayal cannot be beautiful and soothing. This world is full of corruption and pollution. This is not a world for a pure heart. Porter always gives a justified title to her stories and presents her characters who go according to the theme.

She herself says that her "artist work" had received a new impetus through the circle of friends she had recently made, artists and writers and journalists of far wider experience than those she had known in Fort worth and Denver. Among them were Ernestine Evans, who worked for the Christian science Monitor, Rose Wilder Lane, Laura Ingalls Wilder's daughter who has come East from Los Angles; Bessie Beatty, the editor of Mc Call's magazine; Gertrude Emerson, who had travelled in the Orient and now worked for the Asia Publishing Company, and the illustrators Berta Hoemer and Elmer Hader (Interview 18).

Flowering Judas also brings into focus Porter's main tenet of her philosophy of life—that worse than the evil doers are those who give no resistance to evil—the passive onlookers. It is actually based on some actual incidents in Porter's life. During Porter's visit to Mexico in 1920, she met a docile, passive virtuous, innocent American girl, Mary Louise Doherty, with whom she became friendly. Mary taught at an Indian school and Porter taught dancing at a girl's technical school in Mexico. Both used to go together to visit friends in jail and carried cigarettes, reading material, baskets of fruits, marijuana and sleeping pills for the prisoners. Once, a young prisoner asked and received an extra quota of sleeping pills, swallows all the pills together, and therefore, died. Whether, Mary or Porter gave the extra dose of sleeping pills is debatable. But, it could have been Mary, who because of her docile and generous nature, would have had difficulty in refusing the request.

Another time, Mary asked Porter to chaperone her as a man was coming to visit her, a man she was a little afraid of, a man called Yudico, a fat half-Indian, half-Italian revolutionary. He has left his wife and made it a habit to sing sentimental songs to Mary. As Porter walked in through the courtyard, where there actually stood a flowering Judas tree, Porter looked in through the window and saw Mary sitting with an open book on her lap and Yudico beside her. There was a look on Mary's face denoting fear, which planted the germ of Flowering Judas in Porter's mind, where it germinated until it spilled forth, almost a decade later.

Katherine Anne Porter's first published story, "Maria Conception," appeared in 1922, and several others followed during the next few years. A limited edition of "Flowering Judas and Other Stories" came in 1930, containing that first story and in order of their original publication "Magic," "Rope," "He," "The Jilting of Gramy Weatherall" and "Flowering Judas." The 1935 edition included also "Theft," "That Tree," "The Cracked Looking Glass" and "Hacienda." The stories in Flowering Judas are marked by a wide diversity of setting, material, style and structure, but also by a fundamental similarity in technique and thematic content. The earliest of them possess an impersonal objectivity which will gradually yield to increased subjectivity of the later work. Only one of these stories "The Jilting of Granny Weatherall," takes place in the social and geographical world which will become Miss Porter's most characteristic setting, the matriarchal south of the old order. Two other stories, however, "Theft" and "Flowering Judas," have a center the subjective heroine who will carry the thematic weight of the later works. All the stories, as critics have agreed unanimously, display a technical mastery achieved through years of lonely artistic discipline. More important still, and less clearly seen by the critics, they possess an underlying thematic unity which indicates that all without exception were refined and oriented at some spiritual center deep within the author and written with fundamental truthfulness to the intuition they found there. This central institution is the rejection theme, which may be seen gradually taking form in the stories of "Flowering Judas."

Although Katherine Anne Porter's first story "Maria Conception," clearly belongs to the beta class virtue of its semiprimitive characters, its heroine possess the proud self-reliance that will appear late in the autobiographical heroine Miranda. Maria Conception is the only character in the story, if one excepts some of the women of the order, who is portrayed at length and with evident admiration and yet is not at all identifiable with Miranda. Miss Porter has considerable respect for the simple, passionate, elemental life of the Mexican peasant and as in her portrays of the South, she sees the best qualities of a society embodied in its women. Maria has only a narrow field in which to exercise her strength of character. Her instincts, corroborated by society and her strong Catholic faith, demand that she preserves her family by any means. When she finds himself/herself in a predominantly painful marriage, like the ladies of the South, she asserts her integrity and independence not by escaping from the social framework but by dominating it. During the months while her husband is away at war, accompanied by Maria Rosa, Maria Conception lives an isolated life of prayer and hard work, rejecting every offer of sympathy and help from the women of the village: "Keep your prayers to yourself: Lupe, or offer them for others who need them. I will ask God for what I want in this world" (FJ 14). She is not pining for an absent lover; she is, by a long and painful asceticism, purging herself of all dependence and developing the strength she will need to restore by violent and decisive action the family of which she is a guardian. In her this process is instinctive, inarticulate, and obscured by a superstitious piety which gives in air of near madness to her behaviour; yet the emphasis on her self-sufficiency is unmistakable. She is the first of a long line of strong proud independent heroines, and in her qualities receive the approval of instinct, of society, as the story's closing line suggests, of all nature.

As its title indicates, the story is primarily a portrayal of Maria, background and plot serving mainly to reveal her nature. She is a loyal lady who has been betrayed by her husband as husband has become engaged with Maria Rosa, a teenage bee-keeper and left Maria Conception. Later on the situation became more and more critical for her and lastly she killed her competitor, Maria Rosa but adjusted with her husband. This approach of Katherine's characters is mature enough and make us entreated with the crude nudeness of this society which compelled Maria Conception to bend before her husband though calculatively. The austere, apparently simple style is so perfectly adopted to her serene, elemental wisdom that it is sometimes impossible to say whether a given sentence is a description of her or a recording of her own thoughts: "She walked with the free, natural guarded case of the primitive woman carrying and unborn child. The shape of her body was easy, the smelling life was not a distortion, but the right inevitable proportions of a woman. She was entirely contented. Her husband was at work and she was on her way to market to sell her fruits" (4). Maria dominates the marriage. It was she who bought the license and insisted on wedding in the church. Though Juan has a job, he is delinquent during the entire period covered by the story; it is Maria who earns and saves. As the opening line of the story shows: "Maria Conception walked carefully, keeping to the middle of the white dusty road, where the magney thorns and the treacherous carved spines of organ cactus had not gathered so profusely" (2). It indicates that Maria Conception is a conscious character and her walks show that she maintains a balance in her life and avoids the thorns and dusts of it. The hut in which they live is referred to as her house. During the emergency of the murder investigation, Juan assumes with courage and resourcefulness the position of family leadership required by society, but he is only acting out another facet of his romantic idea of himself, and his short time in the role exhausts him completely. Porter presents her characters and their behaviour in a very justified way. As Maria Conception is the main figure of the story, everyone knows that she is the killer, still no one went against her and the police could not locate the culprit. The end of the story finds Juan returned to his former narrow selfishness, sprawled in sleep while Maria sits holding the child of his love for another, which she has in a sense conceived and borne without his help by her act of murder.

In this first of her published stories Katherine Anne Porter confronts the mysterious forces of nature through the transparency of primitive society and finds that these forces met most strongly through a woman. In obeying them this woman attains a dignity which sets her apart from others. No act of hers not even murder, rings false to nature. Her brief, violent disturbance after the deed lasts only long enough to free her from the imputation of inhumanity, and soon gives way to a calm which is not broken even by the sight of the dead girl's face. She is confined and an isolated character.

"Maria Conception"—about a Mexican Indian girl who murders her husband's mistress and takes their baby for her own—is Miss Porter's fine work in this vein. But the exotic pastoratum of that story has obscured Maria's character for many readers. In most interpretations, she is misinterpreted as a pure primitive, who triumphs by the power of instinct over the disorder that the encroachments of alien civilization have brought to her society. As her name is surely meant to indicate, Maria is actually the victim of her own tragic "conceit." She commits the murder in a desperate effect to realise her obsessive idea of herself as a wife and mother—an idea that she has from her oversimplified training in Catholicism, not from her Indian heritage. In the stories having protagonists with whose North American cultural backgrounds. Miss Porter, as well as her reader, is more fully and immediately familiar, the psychological and moral situations are clearer.

Black characters, all of them servants to white families, figure prominently in very few of Katherine Anne Porter's stories. Their personalities and behaviour are of interest chiefly in the way that they reflect, and to some extent influence, the lives of the whites.

Only in "Magic," a very short story significantly, a story that does not belong to the autobiographical series—does Miss Porter distinctly identify with the black woman. Here, too, the blacks consciousness is not directly explored; and Ninette has to evaluate the fortune in terms of the white house holds in which she serves.

The frame situation of this story involves a New Orleans lady of quality, Madame Blanchards and her personal maid. The sordid story she tells is of an episode in the "fancy house" where she formerly worked as a chambermaid.

The ruthless madam of the brothel had habitually checks her whores. Once when she was accused of this by one Ninette, who announced her intention and leaving the house, the madam mercilessly beat the frail girl, with special attention to her private parts and threw her out.

It is sufficiently obvious that Ninette was not brought back to the rowdy house by the power of the magic spell. She came back, of course, simply because she had learned that there was nowhere else for her to go. Porter presents her main character Ninette a sleek girl tortured by her provided lot. She is not confident one as Maria Conception is.

Ninette, Madam Blanchard's maid whose relationship with her mistress is the center of this story that at the first glance it seems to be the work of another author, so different it is from "Maria Conception." "Magic" is unique among Miss Porter's stories in its brevity, its fiercely ironic monologue technique, and the sordidness of its subject mater, yet it is not as remote from the mainstream of her work as it suggests (RPW 42). The extreme of her early experimental and highly objective approach, it is a minor technical masterpiece. In terms of the rejection theme it is one of the purest examples of the destructively oppressive union. Ninette, a flat beta character who contrasts with Maria Conception in almost every respect except participation in a bitterly oppressive union, is pathetically important to free herself. However, the only emphasis of the story is not on sympathy with her as a victim but rather on the horror of her situation. Everything contributes to this effect—the detachment of the girl, callous narration; the doubly callous curiosity of the listener; the irony of the greeting, "Welcome home Ninette," when she returns, the understatement of the last line, "And after that she lived there quietly." The failure of her attempted escape re-emphasizes her enslavement and the ambiguity of her return—whether by magic or merely through the determinism of her situation is a masterskake of further emphasis.

The loathness with which Ninette's subjection is portrayed is exactly the commentary one would expect from Miss Porter on this utter frustration typical of the beta character's plight, of the basic element of the rejection theme; the urge to escape from oppression.

The other story "Rope" is a *tour de force,* a delicately graphed record of a verbal duel between generic "he" and "she." There is a masterful manipulation of elements—setting, accident, masculine and feminine mentality. The whole story is a quarrel between a hurried young husband and wife, signifying nothing more than the instability of human emotions; yet the deep antagonism uncovered by this gratuitous argument; with its traded taunts of barrenness and infidelity casts baleful light on this marriage.

The sense of oppression is built up by emphasis on the stifling heat on the day and the shutter in the house. The husband sums up this feeling as he leaves the second time for the store, after the violent separation which was needed to end the conflict; "things accumulated, things were mountainous, you couldn't move them or sort them out or get rid of them. They just lay and noted around" (FJ 57). His escape is only temporary, and indications are that both he and she continue to stagnate in this destructive marriage. But then, neither of the two is a fully developed character, nor does either have the intelligent self-awareness and intensity of spirit with which Miranda will confront the deep mysteries and painful complexities of life.

In this story "Rope," a young city couple summering in the country fall into a bitter quarrel over the husband's selfish absent mindedness on a shopping trip into town, he forgets to buy the coffee that his wife repeatedly reminded him to get. But indulging an absurd whim, he buys a large coil of heavy rope, which is for no use. The rope of course, symbolizes the invisible bond of their destructive but probably unbreakable union.

They are at the end of the rope of their patience with each other; they have enough rope, with which to hang themselves. But they cannot work free of each other. At the end of the story, exhausted by along exchange of recriminations, they are temporarily reconciled. But it is plain that they are doomed to resume the quarrel once they have rested. Referred to only as "he" and "she" they have, all but lost their personalities in the degrading, continuous struggle that is their marriage.

In the other story "Theft," for the first time the heroine might, both in character and in the concrete details of her life be completely identified with the author. This is highly significant in spite of the fact that Miss Porter is clearly critical of this heroine—because "Theft" contains the clearest expression of the authors' characteristic rejection theme. The heroine is an implicit Miranda, and the story is related closely to "Flowering Judas" in that it is concerned primarily with the over-rejection of the heroine, who could be Laura about twenty years later. The whole story is about the missing of a purse which is a birthday gift from the former lover of its heroine. Between the initial sense of material loss and the profound anguish of spiritual loss with which the story ends.

All the elements in the story points clearly toward rejection. It opens just as the heroine becomes aware of the loss of her purse which is representative of all the possessions, a symbolic extension of her personality.

When the Janitress follows her up the stairs to return the purse, and reminds her of the extent to which she has, with seeming indifference left her belongings exposed to theft. The heroine's anger has cooled somewhat at the realization of her own complicity, but the woman receives it by touching on a particularly painful aspects of loss—the decline of youth and beauty—and by unwillingly reminding her of the loss of her lover by saying that he will buy her another purse if she needs it. Bitterly, the heroine thrusts the purse upon her, rejecting with it both the sufferings and the values it represents. By now the woman has twisted things around to the extent of calling the heroine a thief: "It's not from me, it's from her you're stealing it" (91).

Back in her own room, over cold coffee, she feels the lesson sink in. Once more she has seen herself instinctively reject her own possessions, this time in a parody of generosity which has left her even more alienated than before. She is now painfully conscious of the extent of her self-impoverishment, though how far she sees into its causes remains uncertain. Leonard Prager gives an indication of them: "The protagonist's childishly dimmed propriety sense in a function of a more generalized flight from feelings. To own is to be responsible for, to be concerned with, to expend effort on. His irrational certainty that the world will not take from her is but the negative of the infantile wish to be cared for regardless of what she does or does not do. The form of the wish betrays a fear of feeling and commitment" (Nance 33).

Surely she realizes at least in a dim way that it is her fear of contact and commitment that motivates the principle of rejection which robs her life. She has been sympathetically presented, but one is inclined to blame her over rejection for a large part of her suffering just as in the case of Laura in "Flowering Judas."

The two remaining stories in "Flowering Judas" which are closely related to the alpha heroine are "That Tree" and "The Jilting of Granny Weatherall," the first because its two main characters from a sort of composite, Miranda, and the second because of its heroine implicit kinship with the Grandmother of the "Old Order."

As the very title of this story collection shows about the Fall, Adam leads Eve into knowledge the Father had forbidden. Hawthorne and Porter view the consequence of the Fall differently. Hawthorne suggests, that Donatello's Edenic state was not fully human, whereas his fallen state has awakened his soul and developed a thousand high capabilities moral and intellectual, which we never should have dreamed of asking for, within the scanty compass of Donatello's whom we knew. Her characters often accept their fallen state, but surrender their Edenic dream with great reluctance. We are getting the thing almost all the character of "Flowering Judas." All of its protagonists are mature and compromising. They well know the hard and cruel reality that it is needed to adjust many a times even with the wrong things for maintaining our existence in this polluted world. For having a peaceful security adjustment is must.

Now comes the second collection of short stories of Katherine Anne Porter which is titled as "The Leaning Tower and the Other Stories." As is Miss Porter's writing each and every word, each and every sentence, expression everything has its own symbolic meaning in itself—this particular title too is very significant in its meaning. The tower which is static and straight is a symbol of stability in the world but the cruel fact is that it is leaning—leaning towards instability and shakiness. Present society is so complexed that it has become quite hard to save our existence. There is uncertainty, instability, unpredictability flourishing everywhere. It is a world of tension where everyone is fighting for their stand in it. The title is well concentrated to this paradox of the decaying world.

The Miranda stories contain Katherine Anne Porter's most personal work. It contains much of the author's best work but they must be appeared in their proper way, not as one could approach a more conventional short story such as "Rope" or "He." The six sketches—"The Source," "The Witness," "The Circus," "The Old Order," "The Last Leaf," "The Grave," "Old Morality" are written in the form of a generalized narrative of recollection which reflects the orderly and apparently eternal quality of the Old Southern life. Like most fiction about children or adolescents, the sketches constitute an initiation story. The three which feature Miranda record important discoveries about the elements of life—evil, sex, birth and death, the past, the insignificance of man.

"The Source" in collected stories, introduces us to the Grandmother. Every year, during summer, after school is closed, the Grandmother, with her son Harry and three of her grandchildren visits her farm in the country. On arrival she is greeted by her Negro retainers. She walks through the house, the garden, the yards, the barns, the hay-fields and finally to the Negro huts and finds everything "out of order." She spends her stay at the farm rectifying things—getting the house cleaned, setting up freshly starched curtains and well-well rugs' the entire farm, including the barns and the potato sellers are given the "restoring touch." After this task of the Grandmother is done, she relaxes for a while, and then realizes that she is idling away her time when there is more work to be done. She returns to the house, where once again she feels that things have lapsed in her absence, and once again sets about bringing order to disorder. The character of the Grandmother brings to mind the strong Earth Mother of Aztec mythology, whose duty is to maintain the continuity of life. The Grandmother has all the attributes of a mythological matriarch she has single-handedly raised many children, rules over many Negro servants and is now involved in the task of rearing her grandchildren. She stands as the symbol of fertility—she has planted many trees, which still flower and bear fruit in three of the Southern States. Her psyche is also androgynous, like that of all strong matriarchs.

The character of the Grandmother is based on Porter's own paternal grandmother, Catherine Anne Sicaggs Porter. When Katherine Anne Porter was two years old, her mother passed away and her family moved to Kyle, Hays County, to live with their grandmother.

In her fiction, Katherine Anne Porter deliberately avoids mention of her youngest sister, Mary Alice, because she supplanted Callie in their father's affection. Sophia Jane's-taste in literature closely corresponds to that of Porter's grandmother—both loved and read Dickens, Scott, Dante and Shakespeare. And on reading Joan Givner's account of Katherine Anne Porter's life it becomes clear that what Porter says to Sophia Jane in "The Source" is true in real life also.

They loved their Grandmother, she was the only reality to them in the world that seemed otherwise without fixed authority or refuse, since their mother had died so early that only the eldest girl remembered her vaguely (CS 325).

Katherine's ability to absorb and reflect the past in "The Source" is depicted in the typical Southern setting of the town house and the country farm; in the authentic language of the people, specially the Negroes; and in the individual portrait of the grandmother. The affection Sophia Jane felt for the land and the farm is typically Southern.

The portrait of Grandmother Sophia Jane shows her rising above the sexual repression of the Southern woman. She was raised in typical gentility, but circumstances force her to raise above tradition—she stands as a long figure taking command of her family and her property and running both single-handed. This is similar to the experience of Katherine Anne Porter's own grandmother. The emergence of the woman depicts the breaking of the Old Order. It brings into focus the individual's fight against society—again a breaking of the Old Order as the individual becomes more forceful than even before.

The title of the story—"The Source"—is, in itself, symbolic. It refers to the grandmother who is fountainhead; who sustains her entire family. She manages family and farm with equal ease and competence. Looked at as an introduction to the Miranda stories, the grandmother is the source of the strength and weaknesses of her entire family, just as her real life counterpart Katherine Anne was to the entire Porter family. Both are the symbols and the source—of order, of continuity and of fertility. Sophia Jane—her name is symbolic too Sophia represents skill, intelligence or wisdom and Jane is the feminine of John which symbolizes the graciousness of the Lord. The large straw shepherdess hat that Grandmother Sophia Jane, had woven for herself after the Civil War—a hat which she never wore—represents the past and the kind of life she wished to live but never did. Instead, she now wears a stiffly starched white bonnet—a symbol of the present and of the kind of life she now leads—a strictly non-nonsense kind of life immersed in various responsibilities.

The second story "The Witness," is a description of Uncle Jimbilly, an eccentric and picturesque old Negro who has been family slave since the grandmother's early days. The story shows the three children—Maria, Paul and Miranda—in conversation with Uncle Jimbilly. They go to him with request for a tombstone for their dead tame jackrabbit. While carving out the tombstone he regales the children with tales of the horrors of slavery, which he has witnessed in the past.

Uncle Jimbilly is projected as a typical Negro slave who is now only a servant—lazy, dirty and sloppy. The language he speaks is peculiar to his race. He is extremely religious with a belief in heaven and hell. When Maria asks him to describe "Safe in Heaven" on her dead Jackrabbit's tombstone, Uncle Jimbilly refuses on the ground that the animal is a heathen, that could never have a place in heaven. Irony is implicit when he goes on to relate the deaths of thousands Negro slaves. The white children now want to do the right thing ceremoniously for a dead jackrabbit, but in days gone by, no white man ever worried about the souls of all the Negroes who died in the slavery. His taletelling also illustrates the typical Southern mythopoeic ability. His conversation, though it is his peculiar diction, is also full of Southern rhetoric.

The story "The Witness" is symbolically named—Uncle Jimbilly has witnessed the cruelties suffered by the slaves before the Civil War and appears as a witness for the past, before the three children.

The South's ever-present sense of the past, only remote in "The Source," is here injected explicitly into the Miranda story. It will receive a more complex treatment in "The Old Order" and the later stories. The children's practice of burying animals belongs to a motif that preoccupies the author in several stories.

Although "The Witness," is primarily a character sketch, does not strongly embody any aspect of the rejection theme, echoes of its can be detected in the subject of slavery and the ubiquitous sense of death.

Uncle Jimbilly is here presented as more a historical curiosity than the object of an Uncle Remus—type affection on the part of the children; but it is only later, in "The Last Leaf," that his embodiment of the theme of scorn for men is revealed through the contrast between his character and the Old Nannie's and his disdainful conduct toward him.

There is at one place rejection when Uncle professes the desire to go and live with Nannie, she rejects and tells him "I don 'aim to pass my Las' days waiting on no man" in her typical Negroid diction. In the rejection, she symbolically repulses the present and immerses herself in her past reveries. This rejection also symbolizes on woman's victory over patriarchy, and ironically, it has to be a black woman.

Actually in Katherine Anne Porter's story, the Grandmother represents the past and Miranda the present, when one comes to the foreground, the other recedes into the background.

"The Grave" is one of the finest sketches of Miss Porter. It recounts one episode in Miranda's life; but of the three "The Grave" is the most fully realised and richly suggestive. Though slightly longer than "The Circus," which covers perhaps half a day, it describes events which might easily have occurred within the space of an hour. These events are of the greatest simplicity, beautifully true to reality, and are portrayed with such minute honesty that they come closer to perfection than any other passage of comparable length in Miss Porter's writings. In an early critical study of Miss Porter's work, Lodwick Hartley makes the following statement: "The greatest gift of Miss Porter is her consummate mastery of detail. Whatever may be her structural or emotional limitations, she has the uncanny power of evoking richness from minutiae" (SR 214). The gift is manifested everywhere in her work, but no more astonishing bit of observation can be found than in "The Grave," a simple and tremendously powerful little story of the two children's contact with the mysteries of life and death.

"The Grave" achieves a universality of truth by which it seems to transcend the usual thematic preoccupations of its author. The brief moment in the life of the young heroine is one which she shares in some way with every girl. There are, however, some indications in the story of her special character, which is leading her towards her individual fate. The fundamental one is her strong desire to see, to know. This impels her throughout life, leading her to other pains as it led her to this one. It is this search of experience which takes her to the "strange city of a strange country." The heroine is rather unconventional for the time in her summer outfit of blue overalls, shirt, straw hat, and sandals, but this is in accord with her father's wishes and it is her older sister Maria who is the "really independent and fearless one, in spite of her rather affected ways" (LTOS). It is one of the early signs of Miranda's advance toward maturity that the possession of the gold ring found by Paul arouses in her a desire for more feminine clothing. Up to this tune she has not cared for dolls and has liked to accompany her brother on hunting trips.

Miranda of "The Grave" is not yet very much the strong, self-sufficient one who sees through and rejects the narrow and the oppressive. She is a little girl of nine. Likewise, her father and her brother are not the contemptible weaklings who usually surround Miranda and her self-assured counterparts. This story, is too well-remembered, too close to reality, to be forced into a thematic mold.

"The Grave" impressed upon her the fact that death is universal and may even short-circuit life by coinciding with birth. This story became one of her first steps towards the sense of death as the ultimate and inescapable oppressor. This story carries Miranda toward a wider understanding of life. It is her ignorance of nature that causes the deep urgent pain which oppresses her throughout most of the story and it is the instruction of Aunt Eliza that liberates her from this oppression.

In this collection of stories the thing which is most visible is the tenderness of Catherine's characters. Either the heroine of "Circus" or of "The Source" or of "The Witness" etc. etc., each and everyone is tender and quite unfamiliar with this crude world which is filled up with crude realities. They are innocent enough and feel themselves quite misfit and uneasy in it. They become shaky. But side by side Katherine Anne Porter also presents another character who is mature and understandable as in the form of the portrayal of her grandmother. She is also sensitive but quite mature to some extent. The kind of balance only Porter can maintain in her short-stories.

"The Leaning Tower" stories are the last Miranda stories published. In this group of closely related works of reader becomes acquainted with the social order on which Miranda spent her childhood and with the Grandmother who symbolizes that order and plays an important part in Miranda's formation. Miranda herself is seen in the framework of her family and in her gradual imitation into life. The process of imitation dominates her portrayal in the sketches, which bring her only to the threshold of adolescence. The rejection theme lies behind nearly every motif which recurs frequently in the stories and is almost certain to be found as the informing spirit of every portrayal of character or human relations that is done with thoroughness, sympathy or force. Katherine Anne Porter is a realistic writer. Some of the critics have commented her as a pessimist but her stories well reflect her optimist view and approach and that is of fighting tendency. If we concentrate on her characters we will see that they never surrender rather handle the situation very calculatively. Porter is a minute observer of human nature. She never sees towards the idleness which is not possible. This world is not all a world to be lived but we are compelled to live in it.

If we start comparing each and every characters of Katherine Anne Porter as she has portrayed them in these two collections of her short-stories we will get a vivid change in them. As the characters of "Flowering Judas" are concerned, they are the well balanced characters. They are the men of the world and they well know how to adjust in this changing society. They are quite mature in their thinking and approach. If we take the heroine Maria Conception, we can easily view her maturity in her approach towards life and her husband. Though she kills her competitor Maria Rosa but she leaves her husband and again makes a nice adjustment with him. Porter presents her characters on the real and crude surface of the world. It is well known that for maintaining existence in this corrupt society everyone needs a support and Maria Conception could get that type of support only through her husband and she was well acquainted with this reality. That's why she made a compromise and adjusted with him. It shows the necessity of adjustment though many a times with the wrong things for maintaining our peace and existence in the society. It is also evident in other characters of this story-collection.

The young maid of the story "Magic" again comes back to the nasty place to her crude maiden, lady lord because she did not get any other place for her in this crude world. She was an orphan girl and it was quite tough for her for maintaining survival without any help. She was badly needed some support which she could only get to that lady; she ultimately adjusted with her provided lot. Porter's characters present the crude nudity of this world in this collection. Same is the case with her protagonist in her story "Rope," too. It also deals with the fact that how much it is important to adjust with the situation, to make a compromise with one another to maintain one's family life.

But the characters of "The Leaning Tower" are somewhat of a mixed shades. They are tender and not familiar with the crudeness of the world. They live in an imaginary world. So, when they abruptly face the crude realities, they get shocked. They take time to adjust with it. As the heroine of the "Circus," teenaged tender girl with full of tender feelings. She was quite unaware of the cruelties of life—the hidden sorrowness behind a hidden smiling garb of the characters of the circus. When she saw it disturbed her like anything. But at the same time Porter presents them in a mature way. As the Grandmother of the "Grave" is concerned, she is a very mature lady. She is very possessive, dominating, and also confident in herself. She well maintained her existence though suffering a long crisis. So, Porter's characters in this collection present both side of human nature.

Her approach to the complex problems of maternity and feminine sexuality could be explicated by David Daiche's perception: "Every human being is the prisoner of his own private consciousness, his unique train of association which results in turn from his own unique past. The public gestures he makes towards communication can never be more than approximate and he can never rely on their being understood. Instead, in so far as the gesture are public, they are bound to be falsified the signals each individual flashes to the public world are bound to be in some degree misunderstood by the world, because every other person will read them in the light of the person's own history. Society is thus in a sense unreal, its institutions inevitably blunt and worsen the truth about the individual self, providing means of communication that can distort" (DD 8).

Virginia Woolf's literature also acknowledge the strong female response to various sociological and psychological conditions, through which female consciousness has undergone since primordial times. It seems to reinforce Henry Adam's view: "The study of history is useful to the historian by teaching him his ignorance of women. The woman who is known only through a man is a known wrong (JE 344).

Katherine Anne Porter can well be considered as one of the precursors of this sensibility. Porter had, from the childhood, a fierce curiosity about who she was and what her feminine identity meant. Most of her stories, which have women protagonists, are autobiographical, Robert Penn Warren observed that her heroines search for identity and independence (BA 172). Her fiction represents the woman's point of view but does not seem to be interested in taking an overt political or feminist stance self-consciously; it rather has a curiously personal intensity. Miranda stories, "Maria Conception," "Magic," "Theft," "Rope" etc. well produce a sensibility, whose deeper characteristics are more feminine than masculine.

Most American critics attribute "psychological" as the central feature of her work. But she is neither a doctrinaire Freudian nor has she been influenced by any other school of psychology. It is at the same time true that has fiction reveals insightful and learned observations on feminine psychology, the understanding of the complex feminine behaviour and conflict.

The stories of Katherine Anne Porter, by and large, reveal the disparity between appearance and reality, the problem of artist protagonist's choices and alternatives the pressures of the circumstances, and the state of no choice. The imperfect activities of men and women are revealed in all their inadequacy, whose psyche is exposed to continuous persecution in the world, where self-acknowledge and love have failed.

The conflicts between the characters in Katherine Anne Porter's short stories may be examined in three distinct arrangements. The women protagonists are often in conflict with a character of the opposite sex. The child protagonists are often presented as complete outsiders to a complex and misinterpreted world. The sexual tensions and the distance between the child and adult are often origins for the third conflict, the internal struggle. In addition, other discords such as society, the restraints and expectations of musculature, and inherent limitations are also contributors, to a character's conflict. The conflicts in the lives of Porter's short-story characters serve as realistic depictions of human life in its enigmatic form.

One thing which is most specific in this lady writer and which gives her a distinguish identity, is her strong feminist approach in dealing her stories. Most of the protagonists of her stories are ladies and she presents her heroines in a bold and confident way. Her characters are also unpredictable ones what step they will take is quite tough to discover. And this sudden change in her characters brings a new and fresh meaning in her stories. Her characters fight than to surrender. But side by side they are wise enough and well know when and where to bend for adjusting in this rotten society. It is a quality in Katherine's writing that she presents so vividly this worthless society and still maintains some charm to live in it.

WORKS CITED

Bright, Alfred. *Kazin Book of Life: American Novelists and Story Teller from Hemingway to Mailer*, New Delhi, Allied Publishers, 1973.

Daiches, David. *The Novel and the Modern World*, University of Chicago Press, Chicago, 1970.

Janeway, Elizabeth. *Women's Literature, Harvard Guide to Contemporary American Writing*, ed. Danniel Hoffman, Delhi, 1979.

Nance, William L.S.M. *Katherine Anne Porter and The Art of Rejection*, University of North Carolina Press, Chapel Hill, 1963.

Porter, Katherine Anne. *Interview*.

———. *The Collected Stories of Katherine Anne Porter* (New York: Harcourt, Brace and World, 1965).

———. *Sewance Review*, XLVIII, April, 1940.

———. *The Leaning Tower and Other Stories*, A Delta Book, 1962.

Warren, Robert Penn. "In his important study of Miss Porter's Work—Katherine Anne Porter (Irony with a Centre)" *Kenyon Review*, IV, (Winter, 1942).

11

Mark Strand Among His Contemporaries

MD. EQUEBAL HUSSAIN

A great disorder is an order, said Wallace Stevens. This best describes the contemporary poetic scenario in the United States of America. "Post-war American verse is both abundant and contrary. Styles break out, changing rapidly; cliques form and disappear; poets proliferate. Now confusion, now controversy reign. At times, it seems as if nothing very great is at stake. Certainly no poet, except Lowell or Ginsberg, projects the charisma of Laureates or poetics maudits of another age." (Hassan 88). Indeed, one distinct characteristic of contemporary American poetry is its tremendous diversity. There is virtually no trend, no school.

No wonder, a host of critics view the contemporary poetic scenario with doubt and consider the prevailing tendencies in poetry as 'vacant academic exercises' or 'petty novelty.' The number of poets writing today may be overwhelming, with new writers and new volumes appearing weekly "but they generally seem to be working at the top of their inconsiderable talent to produce a high level of mediocrity" (Gilbert 2). Such assumptions may be true to certain extent but to thus dismiss American poetry today would be more cynical a view than an objective assessment. A lot of poetry is being written, read and appreciated. A number of great talents continue to flourish and enrich the already rich corpus of American and even world poetry.

One of the most interesting things about the contemporary poetry is the movement away from the modernism of the 20s,

30s and 40s into a post-modernist, or contemporary phase. If we take a short look at the pre-50 era, we see that the turbulence that characterised America in the form of the break-up of established economical, political and social institutions, the separation of the self from the history of the race, the alienation of the individual, was recorded most faithfully in Eliot's *The Waste Land* (1922), William's *Spring and All* (1923) and Pound's *Cantos* (1925). Every poet since then has had to work under the dominant influences of these early modernists. Some of them like Robert Frost chose the conventional pattern to the exigencies of contemporary themes. We may put J.C. Ransom, Allen Tate and the other fugitive poets in the group. Some poets like George Oppen, Zukofsky, Kenneth Rexroth, Charles Olson continued to write under the shadow of modernist masters. The third path was followed by a large number of younger poets who although started their career under the aegis of conventional versification, rebelled against traditions and allied themselves with one or the other early modernists. Therefore, the 50s and early 60s were an age of instant 'school.'

A few work out their personal aesthetic, an individual style by which to declare independence from all poetry so far. This gradually culminated into a generation whose happiest achievement has been to join in community, more or less, undisrupted by the squabbles of circles, coteries, and cables. Just as the schools have broken up, the styles of the younger poets have broken out with more adventure. They have become uncharacterisable.

Infact, American poetry is always at its best, as Whitman said of "Leaves of Grass"—'a language experiment.' The poets of the first intensity have been by definition bold and individual stylists. There has not so much been a period style as many styles in the period. Pound had early written that "technique is the test of a man's sincerity" (Hoffman 440) and "American poets, like their fellow countrymen in other fields, are tinkerers; much of their energy has gone into refining or devising poetic contraptions that work on new principles, hence open up untested possibilities to the imagination intent on making verbal models of states of feeling" (440).

But what's happening today is something very extraordinary. The poetry since the 60s isn't just startlingly innovative in the way the poetry of 1910-30 was. It's a poetry without any concrete aesthetic principle. "These poets have hurried to far-out places in the imagination with not so much more critical theory than the need that their images work and their lines be lively" (Lee 6).

Mark Strand (1934-) who matured as a poet in the 60s, represents this new phenomena in American poetry. Therefore, Strand's attitude like many of the contemporary masters of the art reflects a reorientation in thinking about poetry, be it the process of poetic composition, its purpose or, the artistic device to be employed.

The task of making a comparative estimate of Mark Strand with his contemporaries, therefore, is difficult keeping in view the variety of the present American poetry and the uncharacterisable nature of poetry today. Nevertheless, Mark Strand stands apart as a poet of eminence especially on account of the distinctness of his style ('No poem of Strand could have been possibly written by anybody else') (Education 185). Therefore, inspite of his sounding sometimes quite similar to many of his contemporaries like David P. Young (1936-), C.K. Williams (1936-), Marvin Bell (1937-), Michael Benedikt (1937-), Charles Simic (1938-), Wm Brown (1939-) and James Tate (1943-), to name a few, Mark Strand maintains his individuality.

These poet's conceptions of what poetry is, in themselves show remarkable sharing of views and similarity of approach. For instance, while Wm Brown would like to know what he's doing when he writes, (Wm 362) what Strand wants to do in a poem is to discover what it is that he has to say (AC 56). Somewhere else while discussing the craft of poetry, Strand says that 'perhaps the poem is ultimately a metaphor for something unknown, its working out a means of recovery (Strand 347). Most of these poets hold the view that discussions of craft are at best precarious. 'We know only afterwards what it is we have done (Strand 347). C.K. Williams says that he is 'uncertain about everything—the use of poetry, the form of it'

(Lee 7) hinting at the formlessness of contemporary poetry. To quote James Tate, 'aesthetic theories...do not help you write the next line, and if they do that line is probably already long dead' (7). These poets have no aesthetic theory to guide them. It is something of 'a condition,' as Michael Benedikt believes, 'in which all possibilities are open, offering the widest range of choice, including the choice of not choosing at all...not writing, I mean—strikes me as a very spiritual condition' (7).

This rejection of anything programmatic and the scope for unlimited possibilities binds these poets to a group inspite of their being far from groupish. Thus, although their possibilities were unrestricted, Michael Bendikt's and Mark Stand's poetry seems to have been moving in an orderly manner, one free choice pointing towards another. Their earlier works were irregular; in subsequent poems they chose longer verse lengths. Since they weren't committed to any particular prosody, the lines continued getting longer and longer. They have taken the next step: no lines at all, the step from verse to the prose poem. Here is an example, one each from Benedikt and Strand. Strong Tastes: spices in spaces the rear of kitchen cabinets burning holes in their cannisters. Perfumes that hurt. Visions that strain the eyes, sounds so loud they prevent thought. Occasionally, acquaintances who carry around models of cliffs off which you will fall. Fatal secrets confided to Hollywood gossip columnists. Appearing nude on national television. Trust in quick sand. Casts that scratch, a pet plant with tentacles strong enough to drag one under. An airline flight to Arkansas, wearing a beard and long hair and telling everyone about your liking for Martin Luther King. Love thine enemies. Despair of power. A new suit of clothing that walks off down the street without you. Long dream of the immediate present. And the far side of the deserts of deprivation and indulgence, This oasis: One clear glass of pure blue water from which it is absolutely impossible to even recover (Strong Tastes).

I had not begun the great journey I was to undertake. I did not feel like it. At breakfast, I thought of writing to Goethe, but of course did not. I had not met him yet, so would not pretend to be on good terms with him. Would I sit for Raeburn? I turned it over a few times and chose not to. Why should I commit my looks on a particular day to the casual glances of history? I stared a long time at the green fields to the west of the house, and watched with numb fascination, the immobility of two spotted cows. Lunch was out of the question, and so was the letter to Wordsworth. I was sure he would not respond. Would I myself write a poem? I had never written one, but decided that nothing would be lost by postponing the experiment. There is so much not to do! Not to visit Blake or Crabb Robinson. Not to write Corot and tell him about the cows. Not to write Turner about my vision of the sun that like a red cry sank and smothered in rippling water until finally far away the water fell into the soundless chasms of an infinite night. What a relief! My mother, hunched over her needlework, urged me to write my sister to whom I had nothing to say. "In many instances it is better and kinder to write nothing than not to write," said she, quoting someone or other. A day so much like the others, why do anything about it? Whyeven write this down, were it not for any going on record as not having lived. After all, who can believe what is not written down? That I have withdrawn from the abuses of time means little or nothing. I am a place, a place where things come together, then fly apart. Look at the fields disappearing, look at the distant hills, look at the night, the velvety, fragrant night, which has already come, though the sun continues to stand at my door (From a Lost Diary).

Nevertheless, this distrust for rhyme and metre does not prevent them from using it whenever it is required and suits their purposes. Moreover, their poetry even without form (free verse) is as formal as any other verse. Hence, the use of anaphoral and parallelistic structure which are syntactically restrictive and rhythmically binding.

Like Mark Strand most of his contemporary poets have been influenced especially by the numerous groups writing in the preceding age and by anything that have come their way, but the most domineering influences one notices is the assimilation of European surrealism. With the world coming closer and a lot of translations going on, influences often cross the frontiers. This is what Strand means by 'the growing internationalism of American poetry' (Ohio 60). Most of the poets themselves have done excellent job in the field of translation. Thus Mark Strand has to his credit translations of lots of French, Spanish, Mexican, Brazilian and Argentinian poetry. Charles Simice's translations include from the Russian, from the French and from the Yugoslav. Michael Benedikt has contributed translations of many of the French poets and a number of plays from the French, German and Spanish. C.K. Williams too has his own share of translations which include the Rumanians and the Sanskrit poetry. Thus, it would not be wrong to say that most of these poets have horizontal roots in contemporary foreign poetry as much as vertical ones in English. Most of the prominent poets of Strand's period have at least visited what we call the global village. Naturally, there has been a lot of sharing of views which has resulted into the evolution of an international style characterized by plainness of diction, a certain reliance on surrealistic techniques, a strong narrative element.

A whole lot of this younger generation has promptly gone to embrace surrealist modes, rejecting formal tradition even before they practised it, as we see in Strand, Benedikt, Simic, Williams, and the youngest James Tate. "For them all sorts of new raids on the unconscious now seemed possible, new expeditions into feelings hitherto unexpressed because American poets had been limited by using received maps of the territories language had already explored. The poets of the surrealistic mode repeated in a way the Promethean gesture of seizing directly the fires of vision (Hoffman 48). The method of these poets has been very justly described by Charles Wright in one of his poems:

> It will not reveal its name.
> It will not have dreams you can count on.
> It will not be photogenic.
>
> It will not attend our sorrow.
> It will not console our children.
> It will not be able to help us
>
> (The New Poem)

This surrealistic mode is true of any of the poets mentioned above. However, Michael Benedikt and Strand are two of the few poets writing today in whose work it appears in its purest form. For, while the chief appeal of surrealism in recent years has been its implicit breaking down of barriers between conscious and unconscious worlds, and while this is clearly of great importance to Benedikt and Strand, they are also very interested in the sense of the sheer absurdity of human experience that surrealism communicates. Therefore, it is not difficult to pick out the instances of the surreal, the absurd in their poetry. The following lines from Benedikt's poem "Motions" is a case in point.

> Carrying in the black bundle
> The evening paused on the road (Malkoff 60).

And the following lines from Strand's poem "The Door" stand out as a beautiful example of the surrealistic images:

> "It is autumn. People are jumping from jetliners;
> Their relatives leap into the air to join them.
> That is what the shrieking is about. No body wants
> To leave, no body wants to stay behind" (Strand 46).

What, however, distinguishes Strand from Benedikt is his reluctance to follow any consistent mode. Therefore, he frees himself from the influence of surrealism by writing in a characteristically gentle and lyrical mode, and shaping his subconscious experiences with the meticulousness of a very skillful artist. Moreover, inspite of the elusiveness of his poetry, Strand too, like C.K. Williams knows that "we do suffer hunger and love and war. And then how much war there is within us" (Williams 1683). Therefore, one always notices the note of 'a universal anguish.' Benedikt too, makes attempts to sound different but not very successfully by being 'generally witty, often simply funny' (Malkoff 60).

The use of a starkly austere vocabulary characterises most of these poets be it Strand or Simic, Benedikt or Bell, Tate or C.K. Williams. Here are a few examples from some of these poets.

You murder them
They wanted to kill you.

You murder them
They wanted to ask you.

They wanted to ask you
to table.

But you have killed
and have no appetite.

(Bell: Privacy)

In a field
I am the absence
of field.
This is
always the case.
Wherever I am
I am what is missing.

(Strand: Keeping Things Whole)

The dogs huddled close
and put their paws over his eyes
An ambulance backed up over him.

(Tate: Our Hero)

This morning
I heard the sound
of all my unborn children
joined into me.

(Simic: Thrush)

However, this severely plain vocabulary signalling a departure from the past, characterises Strand's poetry almost throughout. Simic too, comes very close to Strand. Like Strand's, Simic's poetry too at times sounds like nursery rhymes. Their poetry appears stripped of everything non-essential 'poetry standing naked in its bone' (Eliot).

In fact, the terrain of these poets being inferiority, the verse would naturally present a barren exterior. Theirs is a poetry part nursery-rhyme for the psychologically distressed, part surrealists copy book for the disenchanted and aggressively adopts the contemporary mode. Like Strand's the typical Simic poem uses a very limited vocabulary, draws plain images from un-adorned objects (stone, grass, knife, fork, spoon bones), and generates tension from surreal lacunae and juxtapositions, while hinting darkly at the ineffable.

Both these poets owe as much to Kafka as to any older American writer. Their poetry, sometimes sounds like Sylvia Plath, but stripped of her pyrotechnic vocabulary and whipsaw syntax. There is a great, great control—a remarkable sense of the poetic that works as a containing factor. Infact, both thematically as well as stylistically Simic is closest to Strand. Charles Molesworth says that Simics's poetry resembles Mark Strand's. "He incorporates the pained sensitivity" (CP 1402) of Mark Strand's poetry. Daniel Hoffman has also pointed out the influence of Strand on Simic's stance and style (Hoffman 551).

David P. Young is also a sound measure of the new poetry because his prosody is usual enough but his images are tastefully objective, his subjects not often bizarre. At the same time like Strand's, the surreal electricity is pulsing through. In "Nineteen Sixty-Three," for instance, there are surreal synapses complicating an emotion that is so of the age that we may need a decade or two to describe it, much less come to terms with it.

The year the President was killed
Was the same my friend was shot
On a Washington street one night
For his white skin and wallet.

What we can't bear we bury.
I go so I thought I could
Stand the abruptness if only
There were some final word.

But when he returned in a dream
Dying and white like Gracchus,
And there was a chance to explain,
We were both shy and speechless.

Then I grew light with wonder
Watching beside the bed,
My stubbornness fell away
For I thought I understood

That he wouldn't elect to live
Here at the end of the myth
If he could, and I smiled and said
"You're the President of Death."

(Young: Nineteen Sixty-Three)

Another quality that binds these poets is the far-off places they have explored in their poems. Thus, there are things happening in their poems, and stories being told, that we haven't been used to in poetry and that might appear shocking to the morals. Thus, in old poetry, it would not have been possible to tell a girl something like Strand says:

There is a girl you like so you tell her
Your penis is big, but that you cannot get yourself to use it.

(Courtship)

So in the new poetry, Strand works the ephemeral penis of "courtship" into a seduction. He does it without any tittering. And there is no bravado when he says elsewhere:

I offered you my wife.
I sat her on the desk and spread her legs.

(My Life by Somebody Else)

Marvin Bell, on the other, wonders "How can you tell her your testicles have fallen off?" (Impotence) (Hewitt 90). He describes a position that fifteen years ago would have looked racy in a marriage manual:

"The deepest penetration, legs drawn,
as if for bicycling...."

(The Daily Grind)

Sex, discernible only under wraps, has been exposed in some striking postures by these poets.

Thus, even a cursory glance at the contemporary American poetry proves the point that unlike the modernists, these poets chose their own paths. There is no denying the fact that one also notices sharing of views among the poets and often finds that the sources of inspiration are common which go as far as Walt Whitman. Most of these poets, for instances, benefit from the surrealist modes and the several groups of poets which still existed or had run out of fashion. Nevertheless, they all being major poets, maintain their distinctness of voice. Therefore, Simic whose stance and style show derivations from Merwin, from Roethke, from Bly, from Strand also, but with the help of French surrealism, he finds a tone of his own which has been described as cryptic, wry, inward, and mysterious. Michael Benedikt whose work is also marked by a definite impact of surrealism, achieves his uniqueness of style in 'his ability to assume more than one voice' (Hewitt 90). The poet uses at least three voices in one of his well-known poems *Mr. Rainman*. He shifts gracefully from his own diction to that of a child to that of an older man.

C.K. Williams whose poetry is marked by deep political undertone 'has extended the opened vocabulary of personal subjects into public anathema' (Lee 9). Using long, prose-textured lines, Williams writes fables that usually begin with ordinary encounter but move from reality through Surrealism towards a revelation. Marvin Bell, another major poet uses straightforward statement instead of surreal imagery, and makes no attempt to probe the depths of the unconscious. As a consequence, the individual is not absorbed into any larger reality—for example, the objective universe of the projectivists, the unindividuated unconscious of the confessional—poets but confirmed in his separateness. He is not an imagist yet, he seems to have taken many lessons from the imagists, like direct treatment of the thing itself, no excess verbiage, rhythm appropriate to the experience of the poem. He presents experiences starkly and directly. Bell tells us what has happened rather than talking about what has happened. Thus, his is a poetry of action dominated by verbs with no adjectives, no ornament. The short lines, the repetitions of words and sounds, set up a tension between rapid movement and futile repetition, which is clearly appropriate to the poem's meaning.

My first wife feared
gas and the night,
and feared the two
would such her inside
out, if she relaxed.

Everyone needed
the help she needed,
she guessed, and she was wrong.
....
I tried to afflict her
with affection,
I tried making her
Knuckle under,
I tried to let her go
crazy, and it worked.

(Pieces)

What gives special place to Mark Strand among his contemporaries is that he has become an influence in his life-time itself. He is the most imitated poet today but the imitations fail to achieve the same effect. Not unlike his contemporaries, Strand's poetry too shows derivations from many a source, the most prominent being the deep impact of surrealism. Nevertheless, he quickly frees himself from all the influences, assimilates everything to develop a distinct style of his own which is characterised by its readability, deceptive simplicity and extreme lyricism. Even in dealing with the inner experiences, he expresses most successfully a universal human anguish which helps him identify with his readers. Infact, Mark Strand's greatness lies in his craftsmanship. Moreover, the steady growth of vision as well as the mannerism, suggests a major voice which has justly been recognized in the form of many awards, he has won and also in his nomination as the 4th Poet Laureate of the United States. Harold Bloom considers Strand 'a poet of genius' (Bloom 136) and Donald Justice declares him to be 'one of the best, may be the very best of the new poets' (Justice).

WORKS CITED

A Conversation with Mark Strand, Ohio Review, Winter, 1972.

Bell Marvin, The Major Young Poets. Al Lee (edit.) Meridian Books, New York, 1971.

Bloom, Harold. Dark and Radiant, Peripheries: Mark Strand and A.R. Ammons, Southern Review, Jan. 1972.

Gilbert, Jack. American Poetry: A Poet's Candid Appraisal, News Feature USIS, Aug. 4, 1975.

Hassan, Ihab. Contemporary American Literature: 1945-72. An Introduction. New York; Frederick Ungar, 1975.

Hoffman, Daniel. Poetry: After Modernism, Harvard Guide to Contemporary American Writing, Oxford Univ. Press, Delhi. 1979.

Hewitt, Geoff. Contemporary Poets, 2nd edition, St. Martin's Press New York, 1975.

Justice, Donald. Darker, Atheneum, 1971, Back Cover.

Lee, Al (ed.) The Major Young Poets, Meridian Books. The World Publishing Company, New York, Cleveland, 1971.

Malkoff, Karl. Crowell's Hand Book of Contemporary American Poetry. New York, Crowell, 1973.

Poetry: School of Dissidents, Harvard Guide to Contemporary American Writing, O.U.P. Delhi, 1981.

Strand, Mark. Notes on The Craft of Poetry, ANTAEUS, 30/31, Spring, 1978.

——. The Continuous Life (Poems), Alfred, A. Knopf, New York, 1991.

Selected Poems, Alfred. A. Knopf, New York, 1991.

The Education of a poet: A conversation between Mark Strand and Nolan Miller, Antioch Review, 39, 1981.

Williams, C.K. Contemporary Poets, 2nd edition, St. Martin's Press, New York, 1975.

Wm, Brown. Quickly Aging Here, edited by Geoff Hewitt, Anchor Books, New York, 1969.

12

Richard Wright's *Native Son* and Mulk Raj Anand's *Untouchable*: An Outlook on Struggle for Social Justice and Human Dignity

K.N. MISHRA

Richard Wright, a major American Black writer of the present times, inspired and influenced a school of writers, changed the course of Black Writers and thus launched a new age in the domain of Afro-American literature. In a word Wright's emergence made the Black Writings articulate and significant. His creative world shows him angry at social injustices, economic exploration, racial oppression, miseries and cruelties around him. Mulk Raj Anand, on the other hand, is a prolific Indian writer in English. He is counted among the leading novelists of his time. No doubt, he helped the Indian writings in English to achieve the respectable status of a rich literature. His fictional world sensitively portrays the poor, the downtrodden, the suppressed, the dehumanized and the isolated struggling to obtain identity and freedom. The creative world of Wright and Anand, as such, represents a vigorous protest against slavery, injustices, discrimination, miseries, tormentations and hypocrisies of the contemporary scene, in favour of liberty, happiness, order and human dignity.

The present article takes into consideration only Wright's *Native Son* and Anand's *Untouchable* the novels which made their writers internationally famous and established them as significant novelists of all the times. While illustrating these two important products of the two major writers of two big democracies of the present world, it has been assumed that no culture in the world is entirely self-contained and that the archetypal pattern of human life is not limited to only one nation or civilization.

It is true that Wright and Anand belong to two different cultural matrices, depict in their works two diametrically divergent environments—one American and the other Indian—the study of *Native Son* and *Untouchable* reveals strong affinities of central themes, thoughts and moral visions between them. The paper attempts to trace out the extent to which Wright and Anand share the same human concerns in portraying the suppressed, the oppressed, the deprived, the exploited and all those who have been forced to remain marginal figures in society by cruel and evil forces. However, in this process of short investigation, the obvious differences in the approaches and methodologies of the two writers cannot be to say that.

It appears important to say that *Untouchable* and *Native Son* are contemporaneous. The former was published in 1935 and the latter came out in 1940. However, both the novels are hero-dominating. Wright and Anand both have made their protagonists very forceful and unforgettable. The novelists vividly and poignantly portray their heroes. From beginning to end, the stories remain preoccupied with their sorrows and sufferings, hopes and fears, thoughts and actions, frustrations and defeats, fights and quests, and psychology and consciousness. The notable point is that in the heroes' reactions—physical as well as emotional—is contained the motifs of the works.

Broadly speaking, *Native Son* closely resembles *Untouchable* with regard to the pivotal issues. The world depicted in each of the novels is a world of slavery, segregation, suffering, alienation and struggle. In the centre of the stories we find a dislocated society. The ugly and hostile forces are seen "full of passionate intensity." In short, both the novels show how the basic right to live with freedom, happiness, recognition and human dignity has been cruelty denied to simple people. Either *Native Son* or *Untouchable* condemns a social system which practices injustices, persecute people on the grounds of caste, class, colour and wealth and thus bring about miseries and violence and disorder in the world.

Bigger and Bakha, the heroes of *Native Son* and *Untouchable* respectively, are not only fully convincing individuals but also representatives of their classes and communities. Both are young, of about the same age. Bigger is twenty, Bakha eighteen. Neither of them has an exceptional background—social, political, economic or educational. Wright and Anand have made a most common man the hero of their novels. Nevertheless, the novelists deserve commendation for turning ordinary individuals into dynamic, emphatic and memorable characters in the gamut of English letters.

The opening pages of the two novels present a notable point of resemblance between them. It is suggested that Bigger and Bakha are outcastes in their respective societies. Bigger, a Negro; lives in the Black ghetto of the city of Chicago. Bakha, a sweeper, a member of the lowest caste in India, lives in the "Outcastes" colony (Anand 1984: 11) of the city of Bulandshahr. The beginning of *Native Son* insists on the sordid and styling conditions of living for the Blacks in American likewise, Anand's *Untouchable* opens with a realistic picture of the colony of the low caste Hindus. And, the picture points out the fact that the situation of living for the underdogs in the orthodox Indian society is entirely uncongenial and subhuman. The racist American society is ruled tyrannically by the Whites. The caste-ridden Indian society is monopolized by the "forward" class Hindus. Thus, *Native Son* and *Untouchable* record parallel backgrounds and situations for their stories. It is noticed how native sons have been turned into outsiders in their own land. Human values have been relegated to the background. The cruel forces have usurped the rights of the weak and the segregated.

Then again, a clash between the individual's psychology and the irrational forces of the environment characterizes both *Native Son* and *Untouchable.* This clash is embodied effectively in the characters of the protagonists, let alone the events and situations. At the core of each of the narratives lies an intense inner conflict working in the heart of the hero. Bigger and

Bakha are extremely sensitive, analytical and self-respecting. They have strong sense of pride which distinguishes them from the other people of their classes. They always feel their estrangement and think about their helplessness and abject plight. Bigger, for instance, is filled with violent resentment to see the White atrocities and brutal norms of segregation:

> "Everytime I think about it I feel somebody's poking a red-hot iron down my throat. Goddammit, look I we live here and they live there. We black and they white. They got things and we can't. It's just living in jail. Half the time I feel like I'm on the outside of the world peeping in through a knot hole in the fence...."
>
> (Wright 1966: 23)

The above quoted extract reinforces Bigger's consciousness as well as his rebellious nature. Bigger suffers humiliations in the hostile white milieu. He has been denied equal civil rights. But he wants to be integrated into all aspects of American life. He likes to be recognized as an organic member of his society with his own ambitions and dreams. Max, his communist lawyer, has rightly expressed the anguish and agony of Bigger's heart in Court:

> "Excluded from, and unassimilated in our society, yet longing to gratify impulses akin to his own but denied the objects and channels evolved through long centuries for their socialized expression, every sunrise and sunset make him guilty of subvertive actions. Every movement of his body is an unconscious protest."
>
> (Ibidem: 367)

A similar situation has been described and delineated in Anand's *Untouchable*. Bakha, a latrine cleaner, is regarded as an untouchable in his society. He pollutes the person he touches, the thing he touches. He gets only insults, scorns, abuses and even brutal assaults at the hands of the caste Hindus. The betel leaf seller from whom Bakha buys cigarettes flings the packet "as a butcher might throw a bone to an insistent dog sniffing round the corner" (Anand 1984: 48). Bakha, like Bigger, feels his isolation acutely, suffers humiliations and wishes to retaliate strongly when he goes to listen to Gandhi on the taboo of Untouchability, he, fearing the serious consequences of touching a caste Hindu, keeps himself apart from the surging crowd:

> "But he became aware of the fact of being a sweeper by the contrast which his dirty, khaki uniform presented to the white garments of most of the crowd. There was an insuperable barrier between himself and the crowd, the barrier of caste. He was part of a consciousness which he could share, and yet not understand. He had been lifted from the gutter, through the barriers of space, to partake of a life which was his, and yet not his. He was in the midst of humanity which included him in its folds and yet debarred him from entering into a sentient, living, quivering contact with it."
>
> (Ibidem: 153)

Like Bigger, Bakha too is uncompromising. He hates to surrender to the unethical demands of his society. He thinks that his sufferings are unmerited. It is for this reason that he resents his fortune. Sohini's molestation by the hypocritical priest makes him furious. Seeing the crowd at the temple:

> "His fist was clenched. His eyes flared wild and red, and his teeth ground between them the challenge: I could show you what that Brahmin dog has done."
>
> (Ibidem: 70)

However, it is important to note that Bakha's smouldering anger fails to come into action. While, Bigger's anguish is spilled out after Mary's murder, though accidental, Bakha's remains suppressed. The outrage in him remains burning. Bigger takes pride in feeling and thinking that he has done something in his life. Moreover, the thought of Mary's murder makes him elated and satisfied that he has taken revenge on the Whites for their brutality:

> "And now that he had killed Mary he felt a lessening of tension in his muscles; he had shed an invisible burden he had long carried."
>
> (Wright: 109)

Why Bakha does not act violently or retaliate upon his adversaries may have social, political or cultural reasons. While Wright's hero smothers Mary, savagely kills his beloved, Bessic, and brutally attacks his friend, Gus, with a knife to kill him, Anand's protagonist remains tolerant throughout. Bigger is temperamental and acts on impulse but Bakha shows remarkable power of forbearance. Besides, he displays inherent faith in God and destiny as a Hindu. He "had often borne the brunt of his misery with a resigned air of fatalism" (Anand: 132).

Not only this, it appears that Bakha believes in Mahatma Gandhi's principle of non-violence. Speaking against the practice of untouchability, Gandhi advised the people to live with love, brotherhood and equality. He told the crowd to carry on "propaganda against the observance of untouchability." He further said:

> "Do this but let there be no compulsion or brute force in securing this end. Peaceful persuasion is the only means."
>
> (Ibidem: 166)

Gandhi's words resound in Bakha's ears for a long time. They give him comfort and consolation. In addition to these facts, it may also be said that when Wright wrote *Native Son* America was a free nation. Democracy had grown up there. But when Anand wrote his *Untouchable*, India was moaning under colonial rule. The country was fighting for freedom and had not breathed the fresh air of democracy as such. Bigger, perhaps for this reason, demands the rights of equality, justice and freedom from all types of segregation more strongly and even violently. Bakha's voice, however, is less aggressive.

Evidently, *Native Son* and *Untouchable* have sociological dimensions. Social wrongs are their central issues. Both the novels show how individuals are suppressed and crushed by society. Bigger and Bakha signify protest for emancipation from the tyrannical forces of restraints and segregation. Actually, they are seepgoats of their societies. True, Wright and Anand both exhibit their commitment and conscious intention, as such, but their artistic integrity cannot be questioned. The progressive ideas are organically related to the incidents and characters. The protagonists, are not involved in any social reformation. Nor do they fight to bring about any change in the social order.

Thus, Wright or Anand cannot be called propagandist as regards these works. The speeches of Max in *Native Son* and the speeches of colonial Hutchinson, Mahatma Gandhi and the young poet against the stigma of Untouchability in *Untouchable* do not weaken the plots of the novels. They rather intensify the final impact. M.K. Naik, one of Anand's veteran critics, has rightly supported Anand's perception expressed in defence of his art in *Untouchable*:

> "In fact, the Mahatma asked me to write a straight forward pamphlet about untouchability. I told him that I would prefer to write a novel, because I wished to present a total personality in response to the challenge, than a cut and dried statement denouncing untouchability, I feel that the novel goes deeper into the roots of human personality than a didactic book, in so far as it is more life like. Creative literature is a mirror. Of course, in my novels, Caliban looks into the mirror more often than Ariel. I have a penchant to notice awkward facts."
>
> (M.K. Naik 1973: 176)

The point worthnoting here is that not only Anand but also Wright has presented such "a total personality" in his work in the form of Bigger Thomas.

In sum, Wright's *Native Son* and Anand's *Untouchable* are great books presenting the struggle of human beings to live a life of dignity. Both the books end on the notes of hope. The last sections show spiritual awakening and moral victory of the protagonists. Bigger and Bakha are metaphors for man's eternal fight against evil forces. The problems of racism and untouchability may be abolished from society but the books will continue to draw people for their human concerns and appeal. Wright and Anand may be called humanists whose chief concern is not less than human predicament. All the deprived, the alienated and the suppressed find a major part of their soul in Bigger and Bakha.

WORKS CITED

Anand, Mulk Raj. Untouchable, New Delhi; Arnold Heinemann, 1984.

Brignane, Russel C. Richard Wright: An Introduction to the Man and His Works. Pittsburgh: University of Pittsburgh Press, 1970.

Cowasjee, Saros. So Many Freedoms: A Study of the Major Fiction of Mulk Raj Anand, Delhi: OUP, 1977.

Fabre, Michael. The Unfinished Quest of Righard Wright. New York: Morrow, 1973.

Fisher, Marlene. The Wisdom of the Heart: A Study of the works of Mulk Raj Anand. New Delhi: Sterling Publishers, 1985.

George, C.J. Mulk Raj Anand: His Art and Concerns. (A Study of His Non-autobiographical Novels) New Delhi: Atlantic Publishers and Distributors, 1994.

Gupta, G.S. Balerama. Mulk Raj Anand: A Study of his Fiction in Humanist Perspective. Bareilly: Prakash Book Depot, 1974.

Joycs, Ann Joyce. Richard Wright's Art of Tragedy. Iowacity: University of Iowa Press, 1986.

Lynch. Michael F. Cralve Revolt: A study of Wright Ellision, and Dostoevsky. New York: Peter Lang, 1990.

Macksay, Richard and Frank E. Moorer. Editors Richard Wright: A Collection of Critical Essays Englewood Cliffs, N.J.: Prentice—Hall, Inc, 1984.

Naik, M.K. Mulk Raj Anand, New Delhi: Arnold Heinemann, 1973.

Paul, Premila. The Novels of Mulk Raj Anand: A thematic study. New Delhi: Sterling Publishers, 1983.

Wright, Richard. Native Son with an Introduction "How 'Bigger' was Bom." New York and Eranston: Harper & Row Publishers, 1966.

13

From the Diaspora: Jews in Saul Bellow's *The Bellarosa Connection*

S. JOSH

Saul Bellow said in an interview: "at a most susceptible time of my life I was wholly Jewish. That's a gift, a piece of good fortune with which one doesn't quarrel" (Kulshrestha 15). The philosophy of Judaism is in his very being, and it is reflected in his works. Though Bellow rejects the Jewish categorization as a limiting factor, his later works are deeply rooted in Jewish consciousness. His growing up in an orthodox Jewish environment has obviously helped him form his Jewish outlook. This has molded his character, behaviour and worldview, and is faithfully reflected in his novels.

The Jews were rarely portrayed realistically in the Western fiction until a few decades ago. They came to prominence in American fiction only in the twentieth century when they began examining the economic struggle of the Eastern European Jewish immigrants in a capitalist society. What drew the attention of the Jewish writers was the painful loss of the *shtetl* tradition as the immigrant Jews adjusted themselves to American life. After the Holocaust, Jewish characters were sentimentalized as paragons of virtue and assigned values such as hard work, love, and suffering. Bernad Malamud's *The Assistant* and Leslie Fielder's *Back to China* are remarkable portrayals of virtuous Jews.

Saul Bellow does not portray virtuous Jews alone nor does he glorify their suffering as Malamud and Leslie Fiedler have done. He gives a balanced picture by portraying them realistically as human beings with their share of virtues and weaknesses. Bellow presents a Jewish philosophical view based on the Talmud which accepts the postulates presented in the Scripture: God as creator and man as subservient. The traditional Jewish philosophers have always tried to establish the moral structure of the world by the application of the holy dictates in the everyday life. Bellow has been influenced by philosophers like Leo Baeck, Maimoindes and Buber, and in his works he has tried to establish their ethical optimism. Because of this staunch faith in the basic tenets of Judaism, Bellow strives to re-establish the foundations of society. He reaffirms the world's need for returning to the humanism of Judaism against the backdrop of Hitler's attempted obliteration of it. Goldman observes: "Bellow's works are polemical tracts that follow certain definitive axial lines of Jewish thought, especially in the presentation of God, man and the universe" (57). Bellow's men are people with human weaknesses who are aware of their condition by the survival of humanity.

Their remarkable instincts for survival due to the faith in the scriptures help them adapt to the new circumstances that set a new pattern of gender system evolved as a result of socialism, psychology and psychoanalysis. When men transform to the new roles for mankind's harmony and survival, their original view of the world based on religion also undergoes transition.

Most of Bellow's protagonists emerge from a religious background of Judaism. His main characters except Henderson and Albert Corde are Jews. In *The Bellarosa Connection*, all are Jews. Nevertheless, their Jewishness per se is seldom the defining feature of their existence. Bellow treats the typical Jewish protagonist—whether as victim, outsider or Shlemiel—as a sort of every man, not as a particular cultural or ethnic type. Yet their Jewishness or, in the case of others, their gentile background shapes their character.

The Bellarosa Connection brings to the fore the meaning of the Jewish suffering and how the Americanized Jews lack it, through Sorella Fonstein, her husband Harry Fonstein, and

Billy Rose. In Sorella, Bellow creates a very strong, shrewd and determined Jewish woman who carries the suffering of her husband and other Jews from the Nazi in her heart. She understands the meaning of their suffering and confronts the legendary Broadway producer Billy Rose who effaced his Jewishness by refusing to acknowledge the rescue operation he master-minded which saves Harry Fonstein from the Nazi-occupied Europe. Sorella is created as a "tiger wife" with her individuality pervading the whole novel. But Bellow presents Sorella's efforts to arrange a meeting between Billy and Harry as a failure which shows his undisguised preference for men.

By the time Bellow reaches *The Bellarosa Connection,* his men are mentally and physically prepared to accept the power and individuality of women. Harry has no difficulty in sending Sorella to Billy as his emissary because he gives equal status to her or perhaps more by virtue of her superior capabilities. Clara, in *A Theft*, and Sorella are women who embody the power of modern femininity while Wilder and Harry Fonstein represent men who are reconciled completely to the changing gender patterns. Men are at ease in their new roles of soft men, and women too enjoy their newly-found avatars of life. With a new enthusiasm and vigour, these "tiger" women carry out their missions for men.

The title *The Bellarosa Connection* refers to an organisation supposedly operated by Billy Rose to smuggle Jews out of wartime Italy. Among them is Harry who escaped via Cuba to America and built a successful business. But his final passage to his adopted homeland is denied by Billy's refusal to meet Harry. By a desire to thank Billy in person, Harry spends some years trying to arrange a meeting with him. Having failed, he gives up his efforts. But Sorella, the "tiger wife" (21) is not prepared to accept defeat. She wants to make sure of her husband's life-long desire to be fulfilled. So, by the end of the 50s, she arranges a visit to Jerusalem knowing that Rose is going there to donate a sculpture garden. Fully prepared with documents of Rose's shady business and sexual affairs, she confronts him in the King David Hotel, hoping to force him to receive Fonstein. But contrary to her expectations she finds a contemptible, sleazy figure who has no interest in the lives of those whom he saved, and in disgust, she leaves the documents there, saying, "You're the filth. I want no part of you" (63). About her experience with Billy Rose, she tells the narrator who accidentally meets the Fonsteins at King David:

> "The Jews could survive everything that Europe threw at them. I mean the lucky remnant. But now comes the next test-America. Can they hold their ground, or will the U.S.A. be too much for them?" (65).

The behaviour of Billy Rose appears strange. The narrator thinks that the fictional schemes for rescuing Jews from Fascist Europe is directly associated with a fantasy he might have developed from Hollywood, "He must've seen Leslie Howard in *The Scarlet Pimpernel*" (11). As Peter Hyland says, "Although his actions were prompted by deep (if vestigial) feelings of Jewishness, he was not capable of understanding the experience of the European Jews" (115). His theatrical constructions are, perhaps, efforts to evade the reality of the sufferings of European Jews when compared to the American immigrants.

But Billy's story is an American success story. Anyone, not only wasps, with cunning and enterprise can achieve material success in "America, the land of opportunity" (43). Because of Billy's amazing success in America, he fails to understand the reality of the escape he had made possible for the European Jews. Sorella fears that the American experience will cut-off the Jews from an understanding of the special experience of their race. When she asks Billy whether he remembers her husband, he replies passively, "Remember, forget-what's the difference to me?" (53). But she knows that Harry's experience was a Jewish experience, "a part of the destruction of the Jews" and not to remember, is to deny it. She realizes that America makes Jews forget about the meaning of a Jew. It makes them forget the suffering that has been the Jewish fate.

Bellow explores this theme in detail in this book. The narrator and Fonstein's son too belong to this category of American Jews. The narrator discovers his condition: "I was a Jew of an entirely different breed. And therefore...closer to Billy Rose and his rescue operation.... You pay a price for being child for the New World" (89). The price is the discovery that he has never really understood the kind of wretched brutality that is the Jewish experience. Fonstein's son Gilbert, a mathematical prodigy, also moves along the line of them though Sorella hoped that the American event will "be different for our children" (64). But the "American event" (64) is not different for Gilbert, who finds a way of selling his abilities, and uses his mathematical genius for developing systems to win at gambling.

Bellow maps Jewish experiences and contradictions very minutely and with profound concern. Billy's religious concerns are entangled with his gender problems. The narrator thinks that Billy's laments on the suffering of the Jews is related to his agony of defeats from woman:

> Billy looked as if he couldn't stop lamenting the long sufferings of the Jews and, in addition, his own defeats at the hands of fellow Jews. My guess was that his defeats by lady Jews were the most deeply wounding of all. He could win against men. Women, if I was correctly informed, were too much for him (44).

Bellow wants to suggest that even sexual torment is American. Old European Jews do not have this problem because they are more connected to God: "His main connection being with his God, he would have granted no such power to a woman" (44). For Billy, the problem of gender recurs again in the novel. It is difficult for him to deal with the opposite sex. Sorella studied Rose's nature and mentioned this to the narrator. He recollects what she told him:

> He couldn't deal even with the slenderest of girls. The least of them had the power to put the sexual whammy (Indian sign) on him. Sorella herself saw this (53).

Bellow's Jews contemplate on their rich cultural history and their Jewishness. Their marginal status seems a metaphor for the modern condition, for the repeated role of the American cut off from his cultural past. As European Jews, with a rich cultural history and an ancient past, they confront the question of how to express their identity. Jeanne Braham comments:

> The Jewish consciousness of Bellow's heroes carries within it an affirmation stamped neither by religious orthodoxy nor by national experience. It draws from our ancient emphasis on the fundamental worth of life and possibility of humanity (35).

The immigrant Jewish families in the United States in the beginning of the twentieth century found an entirely New World which was not in conformity with traditional, masculine Jewish order. They entered a world where the father figure was fast fading reducing the conflict in the families. But in the immigrant Jewish families, the condition was different. They noticed that the new condition in America was a leap in time, forcing new values on the young. Prosperity in this New World could be achieved only by assimilating the traits of it which included modernity, urbanism, industrialism, sexuality and soft manners. So we find in Jewish literature, a tension between the values of the New, which are represented by the son. The immigrants realized that they could "rise" only at the cost of their son as represented by Abraham Cahan in *The Rise of David Levinsky* through Levinsky.

Gabriel Josipovici argues that in *The Bellarosa Connection* Bellow has come out with the new theme of the failure of modern Jews, who "freed of the pressure to succeed, to make of their lives, since their parents have done that for them" (1181) tend to go bad and want to forget their past. If Bellow had consciously avoided Jewish themes in his earlier works, he deliberately discussed such topics in this book. It makes our reading very different as *The Bellarosa Connection* remains a powerful meditation on the Holocaust, the history of the Jews, and the changing nature of the individual's relationship to culture.

WORKS CITED

Bellow, Saul. *The Bellarosa Connection* (New York: Penguin, 1989).

——. *A Theft* (New York: Penguin, 1989).

Braham, Jeanne. *A Sort of Columbus* (Athens: U of Georgia P, 1984).

Goldman, L.H. "Saul Bellow and the Philosophy of Judaism." *Saul Bellow in the 1980s: A Collection of Critical Essays*. Ed. Gloria L. Cronin and L.H. Goldman (Michigan: Michigan UP, 1989), 51-66.

Hyland, Peter. *Saul Bellow* (New York: St. Martin's, 1992).

Josipivici, Gabriel. "The Work of Memory." Rev. of *The Bellarosa Connection*, by Soul Bellow. *Times Literary Supplement*, 27 Oct. 1989: 1181.

Kulshrestha, Chirantan. "A Conversation with Saul Bellow." *Chicago Review* 23 (1972): 7-15.

14

Humanism in the Novels of Saul Bellow

ISHTEYAQUE SHAMS

The present study in the novels of Saul Bellow is an attempt to trace out Bellow's deep concern for unflinching humanism and his repeated assertions to change American social disturbances or chaos into traditional morality and value based society. His novels such as *Mr. Sammler's Planet* (1970) and *Humboldt's Gift* (1975) very much speak about Saul Bellow's faith in humanism and at the same time his idealism which can solve all sorts of moral, ethical and spiritual problems. He is critical of the prevalent American social problems but at the same time very optimistic about the transformation and the regeneration of the people in general and the nation in particular. His fiction gets much of its strength from the character's cultural and emotional complexities, and his idealism grows very much from his commitment to find out solutions to all these complexities and problems. It goes without saying that American morals in 1970s in particular were in disarray and Saul Bellow's treatment of all such complexities makes him very much committed to realism. But it is equally true that he never allows himself to be pessimistic. His optimism very much coincides with idealism, his concern for human regeneration and betterment of society and individuals. He tries to make a balance between man's past and present, a balance between his inner world and outer world.

II

Humanism, in its strict sense, is the Renaissance literary cult of the so-called New learning, a revival of Greek and

Roman studies. It is 'new' to Christianity and other religions and it is a study of highest expression of human values and a means to developing the free, responsible individual. The term 'humanism' is derived from the fifteenth century Italian 'humanista' and this term first came into use in the early sixteenth century to designate the writers and scholars of European Renaissance. As the American historian Prof. P. Cheney observed, Humanism came to many things: "It may be the reasonable balance of life that the early humanists discovered in the Greeks, it may be merely the study of humanities or polite letters;....it may be the responsiveness to all human passions of a Shakespeare or Goethe; it may be a philosophy of which man is the centre and sanction" (C.L., 9). According to Corliss Lamont, "It is a philosophy of joyous service for the greater good of all humanity in this natural world and methods of reason and democracy."

Humanism is not a philosophy only but it is a way of thinking and doing for average men and women seeking to lead a happy and useful life. It is an attitude that emphasises the dignity and worth of the individual. A basic premise of humanism is that people are rational beings who possess within themselves the capacity for truth and virtue. Truly speaking, concern for bettering mankind moves the humanist in the library and scientist in the laboratory. According to Lamont 'Humanism' having its ultimate faith in man, believes that human beings possess the power of potentiality of solving their own problems, through reliance primarily upon reason and scientific method applied with courage and vision. Humanism believes in the goodness of the individual contributing to the welfare of the community. Humanism further believes in the unending questioning of basic assumptions and convictions including its own. Humanism is not a new dogma, but it is a developing philosophy which remains ever open to experimental testing, newly discovered facts and more rigorous reasoning.

The humanist movement started in Italy, where the late medieval writers Dante, Glovanni, Boccacia and Flacesco Petrarch contributed greatly to the discovery and preservation of classical works. Humanist ideals were forcefully expressed by another Italian scholar, Picodella Mirondola, in his 'Oration' on the dignity of man. The movement was further stimulated by the influx of Byzantine scholars who came to Italy after the fall of Constantinople to the Turks in 1453 and by the establishment of the Platonic Academy in Florence. The academy, whose leading thinker was Marsilio Fincino, was founded by the 15th century Florentine stateman and patron of the arts Cosino de Medici. The institution had particular on the literature and architecture of the time. Although humanism developed in Italy principally in the field of literature and art, in central Europe where it was introduced chiefly by the German scholars Johann Reuchlin and Melanchthon, the movement extended into the field of theology and education, and was a major cause of the Reformation.

III

Almost all heroes of Saul Bellow's novels attempt to go beyond human life. To be human is terrifying for all of them. It is so because they do not know what it is to be human and this they must search and find out themselves. Unless and until one fulfils the classic dictum of 'know thyself,' one's redemption is not possible. The idea of being set apart from other human beings is to be done away with. To be more than human is as undesirable as is being less than human. To be sub-human and super-human are equally serious obstacles to the path of salvation. A man who is more than human, will necessarily be less than human. Both deviations involve a detachment from humanity. To be human means to feel human concern, to be responsive to the sufferings of others. Instead of controlling the universe one lives in it, one creature among others, as much an entity as any other, no better, no worse, this seems to be Bellow's principle. The hero must accept himself with all his humanity guilt, evil and mortality. When he accepts himself then only he would accept others, be sympathetic towards them, be ready to help them as far as humanity permits them.

Joseph in *Dangling Man* (1944) is a person greatly 'concerned with keeping intact and free from encumbrance' (D.M., 2). It simply means he does not to be bothered, but likes to keep him to himself. Of course, he has come to realize later on that he cannot reach his ideal and that he will 'have to settle for very, very little.' (D.M., 103). He does not discuss whether war is moral or immoral because he cannot stop it, and he is prepared to kill others in the war if he is required to do so. The question which worries him is whether his life has no unique values to distinguish it from the mass. He feels himself above others, more than others because of his intellectual accomplishments, his knowledge, his interests and his ideas. But soon he comes to accept that 'he is one of shoal, driven towards the weirs' (D.M., 99). The same idea that man cannot transcend human limitations and mortality by any means is brought home in a different way also in the form of a lady selling religious pamphlets which she says, will help the buyer survive the 'maiming fire.' But she herself is ill and thus disproves that anyone can go beyond human weakness or can be other than human.

In *The Victim* (1947), Asa Leventhals' chief burden is his pride. He refuses any involvement in Allbee's disasters and would not take the trouble even to give him a patient hearing. But sometimes under compulsion and sometimes just for fun's sake he goes listening to Allbee and comes to realize that 'human meant accountable in spite of many weaknesses....' (V., 129). He feels that it is unfair perhaps to have to account at forty for what was done at twenty. But unless one was more than human or less than human 'the payments had to be met (V., 128).

In *The Adventures of Augie March* (1953), Augie in his life gets different pieces of advice but one advice which cuts deep in him is 'that he could not be hurt enough by the false of other people' (A.A.M., 522). It simply means that he is accused of being less than human. Augie's elder brother, Simon is also less than human, he first hardens himself to the sufferings of others and then inflicts it others merely for the sake of pleasure. Thea Fenchel wants to be more than human and wanting this does violence to her human capacities. She has only contempt for 'faulty humanity,' including Augie, when he fails her. Gradually Augie learns to become exactly human, he sincerely helps Mimi when she is seriously ill after having an induced abortion. Augie is always at her side. Even his ideal in life—to get married, have children and a small piece of land where he can teach children and keep his mother is like an ordinary human being. He does not expect to set up the 'Happy isles,' nor does he want to dwell with gods, leading a 'fearless life never ageing' (A.A.M., 526). Although in the beginning, he is in search of a fate good enough, by and by he is reconciled to his purely human status where he cannot 'get justice and he cannot give justice, but he can live' (A.A.M., 465).

In *Henderson the Rain King* (1959), for Henderson also, in the beginning, 'it is miserable to be human' (H.R.K., 73). His desire is primarily a drive to surmount all human limitations. He is called 'unkillable' by his wife. In his vanity and over estimation of himself he boasts, 'If I could not have my soul it would cost the earth a catastrophe' (H.R.K., 273). But he is cut to size by the African tribes, one of which is more than human and another is less than human. Arnewi women are weeping unhappily when they see their cows dying without water, but cannot allow them to drink water from the cistern which is contaminated by the presence of the frogs. They are helpless before Nature and cannot ask for anything. Their queen Willatale, can live joyously in the midst of sorrow. On the other hand Wariri are less than human, they force Nature to give them water by sacrificing the guests' freedom, they even do not hesitate to beat their gods. Their King Dahfucan lives calmly in the midst of danger. Henderson drawing something from both, must choose a third possibility, be exactly human. 'He comes to realize that he has no right to ask to have it better than others' (H.R.R., 275). He must live a normal human life loving others and being concerned about them.

In *Herzog* (1965), the true dignity of being human is shown by Herzog. In the beginning Herzog thinks himself to be different from others. He wandered at times whether he belonged to that class of people who had arrangement with fate, who were to be shielded from the worst brutalities of life in return of docility or ingenuous goodwill, that is meekness in exchange for preferential treatment. But soon this illusion is over, he comes to realize, that he ought to be prepared for bad results because he has a wild spirit in him, he may look meek and mild. He suffers a lot and ultimately shreded of his intellectual pretensions, he is purely a human being, enjoying his human status. He sees himself as an object of wonder which he would grant to all. 'I look at myself and see chest, thighs, feet, a head. This strange organisation. I know it will die. And inside something, something, happiness....' (H, 414). It is a pleasure of a shared condition with all human beings. He is neither Moses who stands for religious faith, nor Herzog, the Prince, interested in 'duty and power,' but a human being accepting the identity of being human, exactly and purely.

In *Sammler's Planet* (1970), Mr. Sammler's desire in the evening of his life is to be free from the bondage of ordinary and finite. He thinks himself the human being at the point where he attempted to obtain his rules from being human. He does not take any interest in his own daughter, nor is he concerned with the unhappiness or trouble of anybody else. Even he has shot somebody dead only in order to relieve himself of the psychological trauma of being buried alive. But at the time passes he becomes normalized and starts having sympathy towards others, thus reviving his humanity. He praises Dr. Elya Gruner, who by meeting the terms of his contract in life and even in answering Deaths' call calmly and ungrudgingly, showed and proved the true dignity of being exactly human. In this light, there seems to be no validity of John Jacob Clayton's remark that 'one would expect in a writer who wishes to affirm human life to find characters with strength, grace, even mobility. But Bellow's characters are all lonely, despairing cut off' (J.J.C., 53). Bellow thinks that ego, pride, and the sense of being someone in particular is to be left behind. All the ideal constructions are to be demolished and merely human status is to be achieved before one hopes to be redeemed.

But this search for exactly human qualities is knotty and sadolled by pervasive reality. The human being has to acknowledge the complex pressures of outward reality as well as inner inhibitions. It is their reconciliation to their fate in the real world that brings the greatest imaginative release. The best example is Mr. Sammler who is in search for true humanity has to confront throughout brute powers of the world. The negro, pick pocket, representing the criminal tendencies, Angela Gruner representing perverted attitude, Wallace representing mad protest for financial and emotional independence, all have their claims on Mr. Sammler. But no doubt this very pervasive reality gives meaning to the search for true humanity.

In *Humboldt's Gift* (1975), Bellow explores the relationship of the artist to urban America in all its 'Babylonishness'—calling attention to the burden of 'collective abstraction' weighing down modern consciousness. The protagonist, a writer named Charlie Citrine, is attempting to realign his relationship to the 'reality instructors,' in order to pursue a 'different kind of life.' Convinced that contemporary culture has abandoned true reality for the merely material 'the plastered idols of the Appearances' Citrine is to quest of deeper, 'personal connection with the external world.'

Turning to the writings of 'the famous but misunderstood Dr. Rudolf Steiner,' an Austrian philosopher and the founder of anthroposophy, Citrine undertakes certain spiritual exercises that begin to transform his view of reality. At the same time, Citrine reviews his early friendship with, and subsequent estrangement from, Von Humboldt Fleisher—a gifted poet who has died some years before the novel opens.

In Citrine's view, Humboldt was silenced as a poet and finally destroyed as a man by the massive pressures of a materialistic society, 'the American dollar drive.' As Citrine begins to disentangle himself from these massive pressures, however, he gains new insight into Humboldt's life and career. His discovery at the end of the novel, of a posthumous letter and gift from Humboldt bolsters this insight. Meanwhile, in striking contrast to his dead friend's posthumous 'gift' and 'act of love,' Citrine's mistress, Renata Koffritz, abandons him for a prosperous undertaker. By acting on Citrine's consciousness 'from the grave,' Humboldt validates the message he wrote to Citrine in his final letter, 'remember, we are not natural beings but supernatural beings.'

In *The Dean's December* (1982), The Dean is a humanistic journalist like Sammler attacking the violence and degeneracy of urban life and the collapse of standards, especially among the dirty, rebellious youth of the 1960s. The Dean is also academic like Herzog and must contend, like the latter, with a variety of 'reality instructors,' shrewd, hard, brutal, successful Chicago types who have contempt for 'the moral excitement' that the Dean brings to his observation and assessment of American life. The novel is a meditation on death, as in so many previous Bellow's novels. Here it is death in Bucharest, an 'Oppressive socialist wonderland' and in Chicago, and the protagonist is a man whose tendency is toward an ill-controlled didacticism.

In *More Die of Heartbreak* (1987), the visionary enterprise serves as the focus of the novel's action. Kenneth Trachtenbarg, the novels' narrator, takes a job of teaching at a midwestern American university in order to be near his uncle, an internationally renowned botanist. According to Kenneth, Benn Crader is not only a great scientist but a 'plant clairvoyant,' Benn, says his nephew, 'saw into or looked through plants.' From his uncle, then, Ken hopes to learn to see beneath appearances and beyond the local disturbances of a troubled life. Ironically, however, Ken's narrative records his account of Benn Crader's fall from vision into moral blindness.

Through a disastrous love affair and marriage, Uncle Benn gets involved with an ambitious family that wants to use him as a pawn in a money-making scheme. In the end, Benn escapes to the Arctic, to join a team of research scientists. There, pursuing a comparative study of lichens, he hopes to recover his former self and vision. Dismayed by this turn of events, his nephew appears, nontheless, to have progressed to a turning point in his own life. Some of Benn's 'powers of seeing' Ken avows, 'had been transmitted to me;' He resolves to continue his 'quest for a revelation.'

For half a century Bellow has confronted himself and his readers with the central dilemmas of modern existence. Now he appears, like Ken Trachtenberg to have reached a turning point in his career. 'I think I have done all the thinking that I'm going to do.' Bellow remarked in an interview, "All my life long I have been seriously pondering certain problems and I'll probably continue to do that, but now I'm in a position to use this pondering as a background for the story, and not intrude it so much into the narrative."

If the problems Bellow has pondered during a lifetime of writing have not been solved or resolved, they have at least grown more muted. As the shorter length of his two novellas, *A Theft* and *The Bellarosa Connection,* both published in 1989—testify. Those problems no longer require so much of his time and energy. Instead of Moses Herzog—struggling through hundreds of pages and countless words to silence the 'demon' of 'modern ideas' intoning decline and despair—Bellow gives us Clara Velde, The heroine of *A Theft,* who 'does not take much stock in the collapsing culture bit.'

The first-female to serve as the protagonist of a Bellow's novel, Clora Velde—four times married, thrice divorced—has endured all the marital disappointments and failures besetting her male predecessors. Convinced, however, that one cannot 'separate love from being,' Clara is far more sanguine about human life and relationships. And although she loses heart at several points in her story, Clara is not ultimately disappointed. At the end of *A Theft,* she recovers both her faith in the power of love and the stolen ring that is its symbol.

In *The Bellarosa Connection,* Sorella Fonstein is a New Jersey housewife, a woman so fat that 'she made you look twice at a doorway. When she came to it, she filled the space like a freighter in a canal lock.' But Sorella is larger than life in a more telling sense. 'Greatness,' avows the narrator, is the only word for Sorella's special 'candor.' He adds, 'in this world of liars and cowards, there are people like Sorella. One waits for them in the blind faith that they do exist.'

The narrator pays homage to Sorella's existence by recounting events that transpired thirty years earlier—when, for the sake of her husband, Harry, she administered a dose of her 'Candor' to the Broadway producer Billy Rose. Three decades later, Sorella and Harry Fonstein die in a collision on the New Jersey Tumpike, erased from existence before the narrator can accomplish his hoped-for reunion with them. He reconnects with the past in the only way he can, 'with a Mnemosyne flourish.' Related by a professional memory man, Bellow pays homage to the human powers of memory and the rescue operation it performs against death and oblivion.

IV

We may say that Bellow belonged to a period in American history which is a traditional period. It can be called another Victorian era. Material prosperity, scientific progress and a strong feeling of nationalism had made American outwardly happy and confident but underneath there was a deep negativity, spiritual hunger, dissatisfaction and despair. Restlessness and an eagerness to catch at straws in desperation could certainly be felt. American public became sceptical about technical advancement which threatened the old, dearly-loved traditional ideals of freedom and individuality. They wanted a balanced diet of moral idealism and material opportunity. The writers who could pulse the nation, a group of them, who had largely recovered from their merely negative stage of moral outrage responded to this need. Consequently there came to be felt something new in the literature of the time, which has been variously called as the new nihilism, poetic naturalism, radical innocence, a new concern for final matters, the rule of personality, the disappearance of manners, the end of social engagement and the age of accommodation.

The post Second World War American novels are not so much concerned with social defeats and victories as with Academic fall and Quixotic redemptions. Bellow has been writing for nearly four decades and has been with time as well as ahead of it. He has honestly been voicing the agonies of an individual as well as trying to fill up the vacuum created by the absence of any moral, ethical and religious values. He emphasized that the utmost need of a modern stripped of all traditional, social and religious support, is to know himself and find out sustaining values in his own being. It is very difficult to agree with Eart Rovit who feels that 'the seminal image in all Bellow's fiction is not the image of a man seeking but that of a man brooding in the midst of his solitude' (E.R., 21). It is because seeking and brooding are not antagonistic to each other, on the contrary they are complementary to each other, and specially when the search is something for internal.

Bellow has minutely observed, closely examined and rapturously expressed the feeling of pessimism and alienation in the modern man resulting from the loss of faith, the technical advancement and the scientific progress which degraded human beings. Existence itself became meaningless. Bellow being a sensitive artist knows very well how fatal these feelings could be. Drawing nourishment from great Russian authors and Jewish culture, he makes clear that if man's limitations are inherent, so are his potentialities. The traditional Jewish figures, the Schonorrer and Schlemial, the fall guy and the innocent fool, are part of Bellow's imagination yet the American influence is great on him and he cannot be labelled as a Jewish novelist. His landscape is urban and he gives Chicago—his Chicagoland—the same tragic sparkle, Joyce lavished on Dublin.

Although he cannot be called a didactic author yet certainly he does not belong to the class of 'art for arts sake' writers. He writes with a purpose and his novels contain a search. The problems concerning particulars, persons and time are focussed with larger perspectives, so that they become universal as well as general. Alienation has been presented as a natural outcome of the hero's being involved in a deeper search 'When you go in deep, you run that risk' (H.R.K., 280), he seems to say in these words of Henderson. But, he, at the same time equally emphasizes the necessity of true fellowship with other human beings. He has nothing to do with the fashionable stance of alienation which had beome outdated by 1950. Being exactly human, feeling concerned for others sympathetic and helpful to them is supposed to be the greatest virtue. Only our true humanity can redeem us. Alienation or separation or withdrawal from the world compels a man into a fragile or futile relationship with himself. We might be living in a universe without God, but we still live in the world with others, and it is our relationship with others which largely determine our success or failure as a human being.

WORKS CITED

Bellow, Saul. *Dangling Man,* Penguin Book, 1977.

——, *The Victim,* Penguin Book, 1977.

——, *The Adventures of Augie March,* Penguin Book, 1977.

——, *Henderson the Rain King,* Fawceth Publication, New York, 1965.

——, *Herzog,* Fawceth Publication, New York, 1965.

Clayton, John J., Saul Bellow: In Defense of Man, Bloomington's Indiana University Press, 1968.

Rovit, Earl, *Saul Bellow,* University of Minnesota Pamphlets, 1967.

Contributors

Ishteyaque Shams. Department of English R.L.S.Y. College, Bettiah, Bihar.

Vera Shamina. Associate Professor, Department of Philosophy, Kazan State University, Kazan, Russia.

Mark Shackleton. Department of English, P.O. Box 4, FIN-00014 University of Helsinki, Finland.

Rashmi Gaur. Department of Humanities, Indian Institute of Technology Roorkee, Uttaranchal.

Manuel Brito. Apdo 167, La Laguna, Tenerife, Canary Islands, Spain.

Viorica Patea. Universidad de Salamanca, English Department, Salamanca, Spain.

S.M.R. Azam. Professor of English, J.P. University (Rajendra College Campus), Chapra, Bihar.

Jyoti Mishra. CPWD, Lucknow, Uttar Pradesh.

A.K. Pandey. Lecturer in English, Gopalganj College, Gopalganj, Chapra, Bihar.

Astha Suman. Research Scholar, Department of English, J.P. University, Chapra, Bihar.

Md. Equebal Hussain. Department of English, M.S. College, Motihari, Bihar.

K.N. Mishra. Lecturer in English, Simdega College, Ranchi University, Ranchi, Jharkhand.

S. Josh. Reader, PG and Research Department of English, Sree Narayana College, Kollam, Kerala.